The Jurocracy

The Jurocracy

Government Lawyers, Agency Programs, and Judicial Decisions

Donald L. Horowitz

Lexington Books
D.C. Heath and Company
Lexington, Massachusetts
Toronto

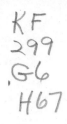

Library of Congress Cataloging in Publication Data
Horowitz, Donald L
  The jurocracy.
  Includes index.
  1. Government attorneys—United States. 2. Administrative
agencies—United States. 3. Judicial review of administrative acts—
United States. I. Title.
KF299.G6H67   342'.73'066   76-27921
ISBN 0-669-00986-5

Published simultaneously in Canada.

Printed in the United States of America.

International Standard Book Number: 0-669-00986-5

Library of Congress Catalog Card Number: 76-27921

For My Mother and
the Memory of My Father

Contents

List of Tables and Figures

Tables

Figures

Acknowledgments

It is a pleasure to express my gratitude to a number of people who facilitated this study. Among government lawyers, my greatest debt is to William D. Appler, formerly of the Department of Justice, who helped me reconstruct many aspects of the Department's work and fill in gaps in my own recollection. Many other government lawyers obliged me with interviews and discussions of their work, and several provided me with the statistical base for the tables in Chapter 4. Joel Cohen, William Goldman, Herbert Kaufman, Michael H. Levin, Richard Liroff, and Mark L. Wolf all contributed helpful comments on the manuscript. Martha Derthick was generous with her comments on the manuscript and made a number of helpful suggestions. My research assistant, Jane Grissmer, gathered and tabulated the data for the tables in Chapter 3. Daniel J. Fiorino helped with a number of last-minute data-gathering chores. Radmila Nikolić typed the manuscript, and Elise Storck typed the final revisions.

1

Government Lawyers: Advocacy and Advice

The government lawyer is a hybrid species—simultaneously lawyer and bureaucrat. He has a dual role as a member of a profession and a member of an organization. Much has been written about professionals in organizations and the conflicting demands placed on them by their dual status. However, relatively little is known about how lawyers manage these tensions, about the extent to which they act as spokesmen for the legal norms articulated by the courts and by their profession.

The legal business of the federal government is, in fact, handled by more than one organization. The demands placed on lawyers vary accordingly. Virtually every government department and agency has its own stable of lawyers. In addition, the Department of Justice acts as a legal service organization for the other departments and agencies, particularly for litigation. Exactly where a lawyer sits in government may be an important determinant of the accommodation that he reaches between his professional calling and his bureaucratic employment. The lawyer who serves in a substantive department may develop one orientation toward his work; the lawyer who serves in the Department of Justice may develop another. How the lawyer behaves affects not just his role in the organization but also the role of law in the organization.

The fact that different orientations may develop among lawyers situated in different departments raises a more general point. How work is organized and parcelled out has much to do with how it is performed. The organization chart may affect recruitment and tenure, as well as norms and behavior on the job. We shall, therefore, be much concerned with the implications of dividing up legal functions in the federal government—implications for the matters just mentioned and also for the conduct of government litigation and the implementation of court decisions.

Legal services are organized in the federal government in such a way that the various departments and agencies are dependent on the Department of Justice for litigation. What this means is that organizations that are, for many purposes, virtually autonomous must, for this purpose, secure the cooperation of another organization. Studies of organizations have devoted far more attention to relations between superiors and subordinates in a hierarchy than to relations across hierarchies. No doubt this reflects what we noted a moment ago—the considerable autonomy enjoyed by many hierarchical bodies—so much so that it becomes possible,

1

for analytical purposes, to speak of almost any hierarchy as a complete "organization" and everything outside it as its "environment." Certainly this has been true of segments of the federal bureaucracy, even down to the bureau level. But where some essential resource resides outside the organization, patterns of relationships develop across organizational lines, and it becomes appropriate to speak of "laterarchy" as well as hierarchy.

Sometimes such relationships are labeled "interdepartmental coordination," sometimes "interorganizational conflict." Both, of course, occur. Every so often the outcome of a course of relations between departments is sanctified in a formal agreement between them. These negotiated documents, dividing tasks or territory, have some of the attributes of treaties among sovereign states. This again makes the point that these relations between departments are in many ways independent of one another. Contacts across legal bureaucracies partake of these characteristics and therefore provide a significant instance of the "foreign relations" among organizations of the same government.

The elements mentioned thus far—the role of lawyers in bureaucracy and the conflicting demands placed on them, the organization of legal work, and lateral relations among legal bureaucrats—are all affected by a force located outside the bureaucracy, the courts. In recent years, the courts have become increasingly involved in the business of the executive branch. Vigorous judicial review of administrative decisions affects the conduct of the government's business. The quality and magnitude of these effects, however, remain uncertain. The impact of judicial decisions on the bureaucracy is mediated in the first instance by government lawyers. In the course of litigation, the lawyers help to shape what issues will be decided, how, and by what court. Once decisions have been rendered, lawyers interpret those decisions. Between cases, they counsel government agencies. One ingredient of the advice they render is, presumably, the requirements of court decisions.

The increasing involvement of the judiciary in bureaucratic work affects the role of government lawyers. As litigation becomes more important, anticipating it and handling it also become more important tasks. The lawyer's overall role may become more significant. Judicial involvement increases the chances that a government lawyer will be torn between what his department does and what the courts say it should be doing. It also raises questions about the appropriate way to provide legal services to the federal government, particularly about whether litigation services should be located inside or outside the departments to be served. Finally, as litigation services are now generally outside the departments, the growing importance of litigation multiplies the occasions for interdepartmental contact and potentially for conflict. In fact, a number of these relationships have been fraught with friction in recent years.

There are further questions that the organization of legal services in the federal government raises for the judicial process. Whether divided authority is apt for litigation at all is a difficult and complex question, from the standpoint of securing the best presentation of the government's case and the best explanation of judge-made law within the bureaucracy. As judicial doctrine is interpreted largely by the lawyers, the extent to which that doctrine actually permeates the departments and agencies may depend in part on how legal services are organized. Consequently, at various points we shall find ourselves involved in a discussion of what arrangements might foster bureaucratic conformity to law.

From all this, it should be clear that this analysis of bureaucracy and litigation is focused on policy evaluation, as well as on behavior. The study deals with how government lawyers conduct their business and also how they might be organized to do so, especially if we attach high priority to heightening the responsiveness of the bureaucracy to judicial doctrine. It should be emphasized, however, that to increase responsiveness to judicially enunciated standards of behavior may not always be an unmitigated good. To do so may diminish administrative responsibility for the conduct of affairs entrusted, at least primarily, to bureaucrats. This is merely to say, of course, that there are questions of goals involved, as well as questions of behavior, and we shall have to keep our eye on both.

Most of the material for this study was gathered during a period between 1969 and 1971 when I served as a lawyer in the Civil Division of the Department of Justice. The Civil Division has principal responsibility for representing the various federal departments and agencies in litigation brought against them, and my work involved me heavily in that litigation. What I learned in the course of my own experience and that of many of my colleagues suggested to me the significance and problematic character of some of the matters discussed here. Having left the department, I set about to systematize what I knew and to fill in what I did not. I reviewed all my case files, notes, and memoranda, conducted discussions with former colleagues, and examined some of their memoranda. I gathered quantitative data comparing agency and Justice Department appeal recommendations (these are reported in Chapter 4), and I conducted interviews with a number of lawyers in departments and agencies to clarify some points that were not clear from earlier contacts or from memoranda.

This study, then, rests on participant-observation, supplemented by interviews and a sample of appeal memoranda, as well as the usual documentary and historical sources. Because so much of the material derives from my own participation or from transactions involving other lawyers that I learned about while participating, naturally there are certain inhibitions on disclosure in some cases, on attribution in others. Information imparted in the course of a confidential relationship cannot be disclosed, unless appropriate camouflage can be devised. Without evidence, however, the basis on which general statements rest will remain concealed. I have tried assiduously to avoid both of these pitfalls, by providing instances of most of the general points that lend themselves to illustrative evidence without breaching any trusts. At the same time, I have tried to compensate for my inability to use certain information by conveying as much of the flavor of attitudes and transactions as possible. I have tested the manuscript on agency and Justice lawyers, former and current. Ultimately, of course, the participant-observer, like the anthropologist who travels to a distant village, may occasionally be forced to support an assertion by simply saying, "I saw the ceremony, and this is how it was." But this appeal to experience should always be only a last resort.

A word should be said about the boundaries of this study. Although the concerns of the study are broad, the material is not equally broad. This is not a study of all government lawyers or all the functions of government lawyers. In particular, it does not deal with the counseling functions of agency lawyers except in connection with litigation. Moreover, the litigation in question is that which tests the authority of a department or agency to conduct its affairs as it has been doing. This by no means exhausts the litigation in which the government participates. Despite these limitations of focus, there is much material here that casts light on all the matters which concern us.

The cases that test the authority of departments and agencies to be doing what they are doing are invariably civil rather than criminal and are almost invariably brought against rather than by a government agency or official. Often they are actions for an injunction, an order that the department or agency should do or refrain from doing something. The suits may be brought by individuals or organizations, and their basis may be an alleged violation of the Constitution, a statute, or an administrative regulation. Such suits may affect programs that run the gamut from veterans' benefits to occupational safety regulations to educational grants to agricultural marketing standards. As we shall see, no sphere of government activity is wholly immune to litigation, although some programs are much more frequently in the courts than others.

It is, as I have suggested, the fact that all programs are candidates for litigation that makes many of the subjects in which we are interested matters of considerable current relevance. Indeed, it is this factor of recurrent litigation that is at the root of a number of interdepartmental disputes over legal services that have arisen in the last few years. It is this, too, that has made some of these disputes matters for policy resolution by Congress. This is, then, a study of government lawyers in the litigation process.

2

A Division of Labor and a Divorce of Functions

The Legal Bureaucracies: A "Laterarchy"

It has long been recognized that every complex organization is character-ized by certain central features inherent in the nature of complex organi-zations.[1] Perhaps the most consistent theme is structural differentiation, both hierarchical and functional. Large, formal organizations require both a chain of command and a division of labor. But it is obvious that how one slices up such an organization has an impact on its organizational product and how it is produced—whether that product is breakfast cereal or mili-tary violence or welfare benefits—and, indeed, on the character and ethos of the organization itself.

What is true of industrial and military and social service bureaucracies is no less true of legal bureaucracies. Our concern here is with the way in which the legal resources and personnel of the federal government have been differentiated and dispersed. The basic thrust of this is succinctly and yet accurately described: The litigating function has been reserved to the Department of Justice and its minions, including the United States at-torneys' offices.[a] The counseling function has been confided to the var-ious operating departments and agencies. To this broad generalization, there are many qualifications.[2] Many of the most significant and interest-ing interactions occur in these interstices. And yet, despite all the caveats and nuances, so many consequences flow from this divorce of the litigat-ing and counseling functions that it can fairly be called the fountainhead of the federal government's modus operandi in the field of administrative law[3]—with one major set of exceptions. As far as litigating authority is concerned, the independent regulatory commissions—the FCC, the NLRB, and the like—are in a class by themselves. They generally can and do represent themselves in court on a regular basis, and their division of legal labor occurs entirely within the confines of their own agency. For that reason, we shall not be concerned with them here.

Most government agencies, however, do not have such litigating au-thority. In court, they are the captive client of the Department of Justice.

---

[a] We shall not be much concerned with the role of United States attorneys because, with some exceptions at the district court level, they play a relatively inconsequential part in han-dling significant administrative agency litigation.

The authority for this divorce of functions is an exceedingly simple statute, as statutes go, which provides as follows:

Except as otherwise authorized by law, the conduct of litigation in which the United States, an agency, or officer thereof is a party, or is interested, and securing evidence therefor, is reserved to officers of the Department of Justice, under the direction of the Attorney General.[4]

For most agencies, whether of cabinet status or not, exceptions to the general rule are not "authorized by law." Rather, Congress has simply created the office of the general counsel or its equivalent (for example, "Solicitor" for the Departments of Labor and the Interior) in the most general terms, without specifying duties or carving out exceptions in the power of the Department of Justice to conduct their affairs in court.[5]

Of course, particular statutes may grant litigating authority to the agencies charged with administering them, but such limited grants of authority are few and far between.[6] The breadth of their interpretation is sometimes a bone of contention between the Department of Justice, which resists the incursions, and the agencies, which sometimes seek to expand their scope for action in court. Nevertheless, as a matter of discretion, the Department of Justice may permit a given agency to represent itself in a particular case or class of cases, with Justice often preserving a measure of control over the litigation by reviewing the documents before they are filed in court. These arrangements vary from agency to agency and case to case, and they depend heavily on the confidence reposed by Justice Department officials in the competence and intentions of the legal personnel in the client agency. Agency lawyers appear most often in the district court.

There we have one side of the coin. Despite all the rough edges, the Department of Justice is the "barrister" of the United States. On the other side, the general counsels' offices are at once its clients and "solicitors" to their own clients in turn—to those entrusted with program management within the agencies. Their mission is to counsel the "program people" about the legal implications of what they are and ought to be doing or not doing.

This dualism is reflected in the mission orientation and organizational structure of the two sets of legal bureaucracies. Lawyers at the Department of Justice master a law or network of laws when it is necessary to prepare for litigation. Lawyers in the general counsels' offices master the agency's authorizing body of law as a matter of routine; indeed, if and when the time for litigation comes, they will usually participate in a process of "educating" the responsible lawyer at Justice in the relevant substantive and procedural law of the agency.

There is, of course, some (comparatively minimal) functional differentiation within the Department of Justice as well, so that individual lawyers do build up pools of expertise and, having once litigated in an area of law, they may find the next such case on their desks as a matter of course. The more important point, however, is that what little functional differentiation exists at Justice is not sliced according to the responsibilities of the client agencies. To the extent that the divisions of the Department of Justice that serve agency clients *are* differentiated, their organizational lines tend to follow the organization chart of the federal judiciary and, to a lesser extent, major statutory areas, such as federal tort claims, that cut across agency lines. The degree to which the Department of Justice is court-oriented is reflected in the important distinction within the Department between trial offices and appellate offices, these two being regarded as quite separate bailiwicks.

Agency lawyers, by contrast, built up areas of substantive expertise revolving around the specific programs of their agency. Their legal knowledge tends to be highly focused and intricate. Many general counsels' offices are, moreover, subdivided by program and subprogram. The General Counsel's Office at the Environmental Protection Agency, for example—though it is a very small office, indeed—is designed to match the agency's statutory programs with exactitude. Hence it consists of four suboffices reminiscent of the Greek elements converted to the industrial age: air, water, pesticides and solid wastes, and grants and contracts. Expertise in such offices tends to become both relatively narrow and rather deep. Often, the narrower the agency's mission, the greater the specialization within its general counsel's office.

Figures 2-1 and 2-2 reflect these differences between Justice and the agencies. Figures 2-1 illustrates the close relation of an office of the general counsel to the rest of the department it serves. For the most part, the divisions of the HEW General Counsel's Office are keyed to servicing the major program offices that comprise the department (Social Security, Civil Rights, Food and Drug, etc.), though there is, as is often the case, some amalgamation of functions within the fewer divisions of the General Counsel's office. As Figure 2-2 shows, the Department of Justice Civil Division, which handles most agency litigation, is organized by almost every principle *except* that of paralleling the organization of the departments and agencies it serves.

Thus, in addition to the divorce of litigation and counseling, a parallel dichotomy has developed between the generalists at the Justice Department and the specialists at the agencies. The "Title II" functionaries at HEW may have their "Title II" lawyers in their department; they will not have them at Justice. Lawyers at Justice generally claim an arcane specialty of only one sort—litigation and the rules of law that apply to all lawsuits or, at most, to all lawsuits of a recurrent type, most notably injunc-

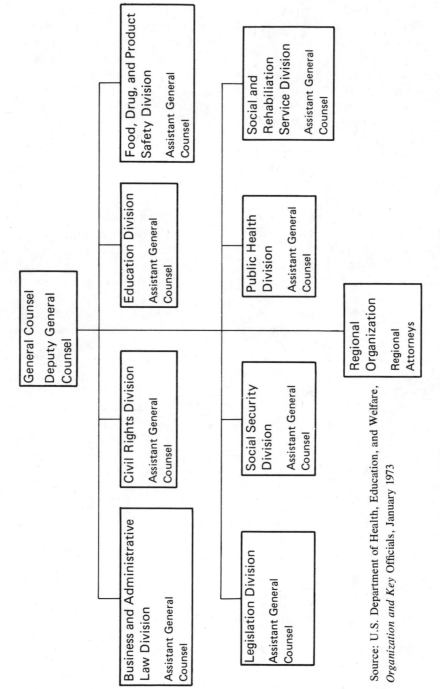

Figure 2-1. Department of Health, Education, and Welfare, Office of the General Counsel.

Source: U.S. Department of Health, Education, and Welfare, *Organization and Key Officials*, January 1973

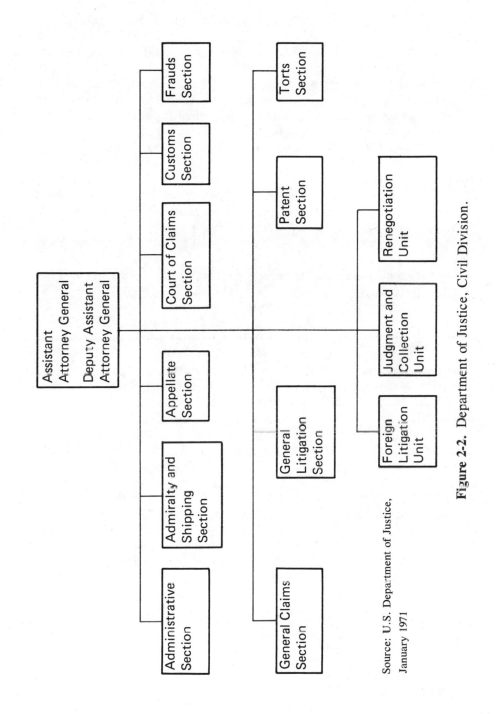

Figure 2-2. Department of Justice, Civil Division.

Source: U.S. Department of Justice, January 1971

tions. To put it more accurately, the assumption at the Department of Justice is that if a lawyer does not know the provisions of a statute or the holding of a decision, he can learn them readily enough for his purposes, often with the aid of the agency lawyers. Failure to know the time limits for filing appropriate papers in court is the unpardonable sin. But the agency lawyer who knows by heart the few sections of "his" statute and "his" regulations, and all the subtleties of their legislative background and administrative interpretation, is no rare specimen.

Of course, these are gross overgeneralizations. There are Justice Department lawyers who have spent their whole careers in the depths of civil frauds and agency lawyers who have handled a wide range of legal matters.[7] But the basic point about generalists and specialists holds, in a probabilistic way, and it holds all the more for those who handle—on both sides—the most important and complex legal problems.

Since the general counsels' offices are integrated wholly into the horizontal and vertical structure of their respective agencies, the differentiation between Justice and the general counsels' offices is complete. Formally, they have no common superior, save the President. This means, of course, that they respond to quite different concerns, and if their concerns were to diverge to the point of irreconcilable conflict, which they rarely do, that conflict could, in principle, be resolved in only one of two places. The first is obviously the White House; the second is, less obviously, the courts. The Department of Justice and the general counsels' offices have, on rare occasions, been on different sides of a lawsuit relating to their respect spheres of authority.[8] More often, conflicts have been resolved, in an almost judicial way, in the office of either the Attorney General (or his deputy) or, more commonly, the Solicitor General, who has the authority to establish the litigating position of the United States. More often still, conflicts are resolved by negotiations, even if they are not called that, between Justice and the agencies.

Most of the time serious conflicts do not arise. The division of labor is, for the most part, understood and followed. The division of labor implies that these lateral relationships (as I think they are appropriately called) are intended to be complementary and cooperative rather than competitive. In principle, neither side is expected to impinge on the "territory" of the other; where they touch, each is supposed to facilitate the work of its counterpart.

Yet, the neatness that is intended may not always be achieved. In practice, there may be sufficient ambiguity about boundaries and, perhaps more important, so much interdependence of work that breakdowns of artificially designed spheres of responsibility can be expected in any complex division of labor. Each lateral actor will, from time to time, become embroiled in the work of the other. At times, there may even be attempts to alter the whole structure of responsibility.

Actually, there are several common sources of tension in lateral relations deriving from a division of labor. Since we encounter them in concrete form in the course of this study, it seems worthwhile to state them at the outset in more general terms.

Differentiation implies spheres of expertise, focus, and attention. If differences of perspective are likely in a hierarchy, they are even more likely in a "laterarchy" where the absence of a common organizational superior permits each party to indulge its own proclivities to a greater extent. In the case of government lawyers, the divergent perspectives fostered by the division of labor respond to genuine needs. Agency personnel find that they have in-house advice readily available from lawyers committed to the agency's goals. At the same time, these lawyers are ready to act as ambassadors for the agency's position outside the walls of the agency. At Justice, however, the partisanship of the agency for its causes is blunted by the intermediary role of the litigation lawyers, so that the courts are not flooded with cases in which the position of the agencies has been unleavened by considerations of a more general nature. Because of the way in which the two sets of lawyers meet these needs, they are likely, in a substantial portion of their cases, to have a rather different appreciation of precisely the same issues.

Beyond that, however, differentiation implies differences in "positioning." In a chain of relationships, each actor has different neighbors on his flanks. Accordingly, his behavior may be governed not only by the tasks that are assigned to him, but also by the behavior and influence of those who surround him but perform different tasks. We might guess that those in close proximity exert a degree of influence on one another greater than the influence that can ordinarily be marshalled by those more distant in the chain. For example, as we shall see, lawyers who are in direct contact with the courts are far more influenced by them than are lawyers whose contact with the courts is more remote and occasional. For this reason, "positioning" also provides some actors with weapons of which others, not similarly positioned, are deprived. In particular, the behavior of an individual or office can often be excused by blaming it on pressure exerted by those located on the immediate flanks of that individual or office.

Conflict may arise for other reasons as well. What has been divided up may not be entirely divisible, or what was once divisible may now be much less so. There may also be differing interpretations of how responsibilities actually *have* been divided up. These sources of conflict may intersect if the work to be divided begins to look less and less divisible and the apportionment of responsibility either contains room for ambiguity or looks so senselessly rigid as to lose its legitimacy in the face of changing circumstances.

Occasionally, too, one of the flank actors may be so powerful as to induce the center actor to alter his own mission and even to attempt to alter the views and behavior of the actor on the *other* flank. As we shall see, changing conceptions of judicial review have put the courts in the position of being the flank actors responsible for much of the conflict between the two sets of government lawyers.

There is also the possibility, obvious yet easily overlooked, that one side will simply find the work of the other side more attractive than its own work, or that it will be dissatisfied with the way in which its counterpart is doing its job. When this happens, there may be attempts to overthrow the division of labor. More than one such attempt, deriving in part from the attractiveness of litigation to lawyers, has been made by agencies in the recent past. These are discussed in Chapter 6.

Given the sensitivity of the whole chain to change at any point, significant changes in relationships all along the way may be expected when one actor alters its behavior appreciably. Such an alteration—in this case in the nature and significance of judicial review—now threatens with obsolescence the time-honored division of labor between counselors and litigators.

The Origins of the Divorce

The dispersion of legal functions among various offices in the federal government has a long pedigree. The office of Attorney General was created by the Judiciary Act of 1789. The Attorney General was to represent the United States in the Supreme Court, as well as to render legal advice to the heads of the federal departments. The same statute provided for the appointment of United States district attorneys for each of the federal district courts that the act also established. The district attorneys were given authority to ''prosecute in such district all delinquents for crimes and offenses cognizable under the authority of the United States, and all civil actions in which the United States shall be concerned.''[9] Nowhere, however, was the Attorney General given supervisory power over the district attorneys; nor was authority to control government litigation in the lower courts reserved to the Attorney General or prohibited to the executive departments involved in the litigation. The Attorney General could not have assumed such powers in any event: his was a one-man office.

From the very beginning, there was thus geographic and functional differentiation. What quickly evolved was a tripartite division of authority that is, in some measure, recognizable even today. The Attorney General worked at the apex of the system, in the Supreme Court and the Cabinet. The district attorneys controlled all matters in the lower courts, but after 1830 subject to the power of the Solicitor of the Treasury to instruct them "in all matters and proceedings appertaining to suits in which the United States is a party or interested."[10] The cabinet departments, meanwhile, went very much their own way, employing district attorneys or outside counsel, as it suited them, to represent them in the courts.

This diffuse structure was at various times recognized, ratified, and modified by Congress, which repeatedly rejected proposals to create a unified "law department" for the federal government.[11] In 1836 Congress conferred power on the Auditor of the Post Office Department to take legal action to collect debts owed the department,[12] and in 1853 Congress explicitly provided that the head of a department could, in his discretion, employ special counsel in behalf of the government.[13]

There matters stood until 1861, when Congress took the first step toward centralizing control over the government's legal business. The Attorney General was given power over the district attorneys, but this control proved to be only nominal; an explanatory act preserving the powers of the Solicitor of the Treasury followed in short order.[14]

Meanwhile, the executive departments had proliferated, and with them the number of legal officers. Once again Congress became concerned about lack of uniformity and even conflicting legal opinions from department to department.[15] In 1870, therefore, it enacted a statute that created for the first time a Department of Justice around the existing structure of the Attorney General's office.[16] This statute is the forebear of the statutes that presently define the litigating authority of the Justice Department. With the Attorney General at its head, the Department was to assume control over all the government's legal business, advice as well as advocacy. The various solicitors of the departments were transferred to the Department of Justice, for that department was to service all the executive agencies. The departments were also prohibited from retaining outside counsel without the approval of the Attorney General. The district attorneys, too, were placed under the supervision of the Attorney General, and from that point on relations between Justice and the other departments and agencies were no longer entwined in the other great division of authority, between Washington and the districts.

The act was sweeping, because Congress had discovered two things of which it thoroughly disapproved: divergent legal opinions from department to department, and even certain "law officers [who], being subject to the control of the heads of the departments, in some instances give advice which seems to have been instigated by the heads of the departments, or at least advice which seems designed to strengthen the resolution to which the head of the department may have come in a particular instance."[17] These twin problems—lack of uniformity and the existence of parochialism in the departments—were to constitute enduring themes in the decades to come.

Having taken firm control, Congress soon relaxed its grip again. In practice, departmental law officers often proved difficult for the Attorney General to control, and new legal positions were created without making them subject to the authority of the Department of Justice;[18] a wartime attempt in 1918 to subject all agency lawyers to the authority of the Department of Justice proved short-lived.[19] Some agencies began to conduct their own litigation. By the late 1920s there were more than 900 legal positions in the federal government, the vast majority of them quite independent of the Justice Department.[20] The 1870 law had failed.[21]

By the time of the New Deal, the conditions of 1870 had returned. The pendulum was due to swing back, and it did; but this time no attempt was made to consolidate all the legal work of the various federal departments and agencies in the Department of Justice. Instead, the line was drawn at litigation. The President issued an executive order transferring all litigating authority—but *only* litigating authority—to the Department of Justice and providing Justice with discretion to decide how and whether to prosecute or defend all government litigation.[22] This is the clearest statement of the Justice Department monopoly of litigating authority.

These arrangements have not always been adhered to scrupulously. In the New Deal period, ad hoc agreements were sometimes worked out between the Justice Department and some of the newer agencies that allowed the latter to participate in litigation "subject to the direction and control of the Attorney General." In practice, that direction and control was often not exercised, and so some agencies again had de facto litigating authority that in some areas has persisted unimpaired over the years.

For the most part, however, the New Deal consolidation has survived. There has not been a general swing of the pendulum back to the agencies.[23] In part, no doubt, this is because the executive order did not also attempt to do the impossible—to vest the counseling function in the Department of Justice at a time when the number of federal agencies and programs and the complexities of their tasks were growing enormously. The division of labor in its present form thus dates back to 1933.

The Divorce and the Courts: First Phase

In what may seem to be the dim, distant past of a few decades ago, there was a time when most government agencies, like most private corporations, could expect to manage their own affairs free from the interference of the courts and the wider publics the courts tend to represent. Litigation was, if not an aberration, at least an exception; it was certainly not part of the daily business of most government agencies. When it happened, the agency lawyers could entrust the lawsuit to the Department of Justice, confident of a favorable outcome in the vast majority of cases.

Indeed, in most cases, as I have said, the agency had a more than fair bet that the substance of the complaint underlying the suit would not be heard. The trinity of standard government defenses—no jurisdiction, no standing to sue, and failure to exhaust administrative remedies (that is, agency procedures for redress of grievances)—was ordinarily sufficient to avoid a judicial decision that actually reached the merits of the challenged agency action. If all else failed, the "substantial evidence" rule could be invoked to defeat the challenge. That is to say, the courts would not intervene to judge the validity of agency action if there was substantial evidence (more than a "scintilla," less than a "preponderance") to support it, even if a court, looking at the matter afresh, might have weighed the evidence differently and reached an opposite result from the one reached by the agency. Some agency actions were (and, in principle, still are) reviewable only if it could be shown that the action was "arbitrary, capricious or unreasonable"—which is to say only if no reason, however, shadowy, could be adduced to support it. All these doctrines—and others that could be cited—stood between the agency and judicial intrusion into its concerns.

These doctrines were underpinned by—and in turn reinforced—a formidable congeries of myths and assumptions. They dated from the heady days of confidence in the new technique of administrative regulation as a way of managing the new burdens assumed by the regulatory and later the service state.[24] The agencies were specialists and, as such, possessed putative expertise which courts were loath to override. Moreover, the business of the agencies was not strictly "legal," and courts were in the law business and that business only. Paradoxically, that very notion, which had earlier given rise to grave doubts about the wisdom and constitutionality of delegating wide authority to agencies, was later to prove the strongest support of agency immunity from judicial intervention.

Nor were these myths and assumptions mere figments of the imagination of lawyers. They were supported by the experience of the New Deal agencies and, even more, of the wartime agencies. Why should a court meddle in the affairs of people who seemed possessed of a formidable capacity to "get things done"? Why, especially when to do so not only would increase the judicial work load in unfamiliar areas, but also would violate the more general canon of judicial self-restraint?

While these conditions prevailed, litigation could be regarded as no part of the agencies' routine business.[b] Cases that arose could be referred

---

[b]This was true with the exception of the infancy of new agencies or of new programs in old agencies, when broad challenges (often on constitutional grounds) to their statutory authority or their regulations could be expected. Once these basic questions were resolved, agency lawyers generally settled down to the routine business of counseling. Often this transition in the life cycle of the agency, from "infancy" to "maturity," was accompanied by changes in personnel, as the excitement of the formative phase receded.

to Justice, secure in the expectation of either a favorable result or, in those few cases where the result was unfavorable, a decision that would be modest in its implications and relatively easy to adapt to. The agency and its lawyers could attend to the agency's business, and the Justice Department could handle the courts on their own self-denying terms. The divorce was, in short, well suited to the conditions of the first six decades or so of the twentieth century.

The Divorce and the Courts: A New Phase

These conditions no longer obtain. Over the last decade or so, there has been a tendency toward more searching judicial review of administrative action. Confidence in "administration" has yielded to cynicism about "bureaucracy." In spite of this, more and more responsibilities have been entrusted to administrative authority, and the courts have seen enough abuses of authority to recognize the need for a more active judicial role in administrative oversight. More than occasionally, the expertise of the agencies has appeared to judges to cover over their failings and foibles. New interest groups have also arisen to challenge the totality of the agencies' control over their own bailiwicks,[c] and they have armed themselves with battalions of innovative lawyers able to bring out the heavy artillery to pierce the armor of agency practice and antique legal doctrine. Some of the new responsibilities of the agencies have been aimed at neither mere regulation nor even social service but rather at social change, and courts have grown impatient on those occasions when they have perceived, accurately or not, no change.

As all this was happening, the federal courts were becoming more activist across the board, and administrative action also fell in the line of fire. As agencies had earlier learned that they could purchase immunity from judicial penetration by invoking defenses like failure to exhaust administrative remedies, they, not unnaturally, invoked them with excessive zeal and cheapened their currency. And so, for all these reasons and more, jurisdiction has been expanding, standing to sue has been conferred on additional classes of plaintiffs, and the failure of a litigant to exhaust an

[c] There has been a steady increase in the number of suits brought by nonprofit organizations to challenge agency action. This was evident from a sample of parties plaintiff in 857 agency cases in the federal district courts and courts of appeals (excluding certain categories of heavily routine cases—tort claims, Social Security, National Service Life Insurance, and Bureau of Employee Compensation appeals—and cases related to the Vietnam war), in the early 1950s, early 1960s, and early 1970s. In all three periods, business firms were consistently plaintiffs in about one-fourth of all cases, while individual plaintiffs declined from 72 percent in the 1950s to 63 percent in the 1960s, and 49 percent in the 1970s. Nonprofit organizations were plaintiffs in 1 to 2 percent of the litigation challenging agency action ten or twenty years ago, but in 23 percent in the early 1970s.

administrative remedy has been more and more frequently excused by the courts. As chinks have been exposed in the government's procedural armor, the courts have increasingly reached the merits of the challenged administrative action.

This has happened despite the Administrative Procedure Act of 1946,[25] which, for quite some time, shielded the agencies from extensive judicial involvement in their business. The APA provided procedural rules for agencies to follow and made certain administrative decisions subject to judicial review. But resort to the courts was possible in the vast majority of cases only when a showing of procedural irregularity was made. Rarely was it possible to challenge administrative action in court on substantive grounds—that is, by showing that, though an agency had acted in accordance with established procedures, it had nonetheless reached an inappropriate resolution of the problem before it. The APA contained a blanket exception to judicial review for matters "committed to agency discretion." The courts were not to second-guess wholly discretionary judgments. Nor were they to overturn agency action if the agency had followed the appropriate procedure, unless the action was "arbitrary, capricious, an abuse of discretion, or otherwise not in accordance with law" or "unsupported by substantial evidence," even though the reviewing court, were it empowered to decide the controversy for itself, might reach a different result.[26]

These strictures, apt for a time of national quiescence and deference to expertise, have in large measure given way before a new spirit of skepticism and disdain for excessive specialization. The judges have come to be regarded as expediters dissolving the sediment that has accumulated on the administrative machine. Courts now find themselves judging "feasibility" and "prudence"—exactly the matters once thought to be the sole province of administrators—and weighing the costs and benefits of administrative decisions.[27] Judicial opinions are replete with language about the need for "thorough, probing, in-depth" review of administrative decisions.[28] The exceptions to judicial review for "matters committed to agency discretion" has been narrowly confined.[29] There is a new willingness to probe into what the agencies have done.

This intervention in the affairs of administrative agencies does not spring from the same distrust of government that says "nothing works," but from a meliorist view that argues that things can be *made* to work if only matters are judged "on their merits." And that, of course, is where the special experience of the judges becomes relevant. In the eyes of the most activist judges, what is involved is a "fight to limit discretion" on the part of administrative agencies, in the name of "rational and permissible rule[s] of decision."[30] To attempt this, of course, is to be involved in the merits of administrative decisions.

With the merits opened more readily to judicial scrutiny, the scope of redress has also widened. If an agency now loses a lawsuit challenging one of its major programs, it can no longer be assured of an easy postlitigation adaptation. Instead it may be confronted with a detailed injunction. As in other fields, when the courts find "illegal action," they are occasionally prone to redress it with orders they regard as sweeping enough to set things aright and to guard against recurrence.

One consequence of all this has been literally to put the government on the defensive. Since 1941, the number of civil cases in which the United States or one of its agencies was a plaintiff in the federal district courts has remained remarkably constant (averaging 13,000 to 14,000 per annum), whereas cases in which it has been a defendant have increased markedly in each decade (Table 2–1). From 1961 to 1971 alone, there was a doubling of cases in which the United States was a defendant. Some of the increase is attributable to the expanded number of prisoners' petitions and tort claims suits, two clearly classified categories that have registered substantial increases. But, even with prison matters excluded, the figures are impressive (Table 2–2).

While it is not easy to determine how much of the increase is accounted for by challenges to administrative agency action, the aggregate figures and a sampling of reported cases suggest that the increase in suits against agencies is formidable.[d] Suing government agencies to challenge what they have done and how they have gone about doing it has become a matter of routine. So customary has it become to defend agency action in court that a recent annual report of the Attorney General, explaining a per annum increase of 2278 cases handled by the office defending most agency cases at the trial court level, remarks almost offhandedly that "In part, this increase reflects the substantial expansion of litigation brought under recently-enacted statutes such as the Food Stamp Acts, the Medicare and Medicaid Act and various other welfare statutes."[31] Create a program and the lawsuits will follow close behind.

The circumstances and doctrines that made the divorce of litigating and counseling easy to accept have thus been eroded. Virtually every agency must now regard litigation as a significant element in its business. In a recent annual report, the Civil Service Commission, reviewing just the "highlights" of court decisions affecting its work, listed cases touching on the job-relatedness of examinations for entry, racial discrimination and preferential hiring, political activities of employees, employment of homosexuals, procedure in discipline cases, and the eligibility of aliens for entry into government service. Again, these were just the highlights! If

---

[d] In the sample referred to in note c, the average per annum number of reported district court cases challenging agency action (with the exclusions mentioned) had increased more than sixfold between the early 1950s and the early 1970s.

Table 2-1

Cases Filed by and against the United States, Its Agencies, and Officials, in District Court, 1941-71

Year	U.S. Plaintiff	U.S. Defendant	Total
1941	12,656	1,888	14,544
1951	15,097	4,327	19,424
1961	13,816	6,027	19,843
1971	13,183	11,903	25,086

Source: *Annual Report of the Director of the Administrative Office of United States Courts*: 1941, pp. 95-96; 1951, pp. 130-31; 1961, p. 238; 1971, p. 262.

Table 2-2

District Court Judgments Entered in Civil Cases to which the United States Was a Party (Prison Matters Excluded)

1962	1964	1966	1968	1970	1972
4838	5385	5711	6321	9706	10,812

Source: Paul D. Carrington, "United States Civil Appeals" (paper prepared for the Administrative Conference of the United States and the Federal Judicial Center, Feb. 28, 1973; mimeo), p. 22.

a mail carrier is dismissed from his job for conducting an extramarital affair; if the Federal Highway Administration approves a new interstate route, or the AEC a power plant; if cadets at the military academies are required to attend Sunday chapel; if the Environmental Protection Agency suspends the registration of a pesticide; if the Department of Transportation requires air bags to be installed in all new automobiles; if HUD authorizes mortgage insurance for a new low-income housing project; if HEW construes its grant-making authority under the Elementary and Secondary Education Act to permit grants to church-related schools; or if the Department of Agriculture regulations allow deductions from the wages of migrant farm laborers without violating the minimum-wage provisions of the Sugar Act—if today, any of these orders and omissions are chargeable to the agency, they can no longer be regarded, as they once were, as residing within the scope of "administrative discretion" or shielded from judicial review by the panoply of procedural rules that barred litigants at the threshold of the courthouse door.

Clearly, these developments alter the problems of agency officials and the lawyers who represent them. It has become far more important for both to be able to anticipate the judicial response to proposed administrative action and no less important to be able to convey to the courts, with a degree of accuracy and detail that earlier would have been quite superfluous, the goals and the thrust of action accomplished or in progress.

Equally important, the judicial decisions that emerge from such controversies will ramify throughout the administrative system. The same decision will often have implications for more than one agency, and it will almost surely be followed by further litigation in the same area. The rules of the game, which fostered the divorce of litigation from counseling, have been changed, and changed drastically.

Keeping the Divorce Alive

If the divorce is no longer so comfortable, what continues to sustain it? The easy and not wholly inaccurate answer is, of course, sheer inertia. Neither the Department of Justice nor the agencies has fully reacted to the qualitatively new conditions that prevail. For one thing, the impact of what might be called the new constellation of judicial forces acting on the agencies and their programs has been uneven by agency and by program, so that the need for an across-the-board rethinking has been less than glaringly obvious to the participants. In addition, the continuing and accelerating flow of litigation makes "policy planning and coordination," so often anathema to case-trained lawyers, appear to be a real deviation from the primary mission of the Justice Department.

Indeed, the quickening flow of cases has had the opposite effect. It has tended to keep Justice so busy on the litigation end of things that institutionalizing a general counseling role for it would be quite unthinkable, even though that very flow of cases may be partly the product of inadequate counseling to avert litigation.[32] The principal response (easy to justify with a rapidly growing case load) has simply been staff expansion. Furthermore, litigation is so highly ritualized—what with court-imposed deadlines and the like—that any reordering is likely to prove to be a massive undertaking, with unpredictable consequences for relations between the government-as-litigant and the courts.

The continuing viability of the divorce cannot be attributed wholly to institutional lag, however. Advocacy is so natural a function for a fully socialized lawyer that the representative role is an independent source of support for the divorce.[33] That is not to say that the Justice Department lawyers are not skeptical of many of the causes they espouse in their role as advocates. Quite the contrary. Many of them entertain frequent and serious doubts about the propriety of the agency action they are called upon to defend. Conversely, they take satisfaction, whenever they can, from being on what they regard as "the right side" of a lawsuit. But the ideology of the adversary process constitutes a powerful shield against self-doubt in litigation. If the truth will out after strenuous combat in court, then there is no necessary reason why the truth must prevail in advance of that combat. The government loses enough cases to reassure its advocates that the adversary system is working—that if they defend the indefensible, the weakness of their position will be exposed and arbitrary agency action will be corrected at some stage of the litigation. The extent to which arbitrariness goes unredressed can be attributed to slippage in the system, which, for all its faults, is still perceived as virtuous. Whatever their personal views on the legal merits of the way a given program is administered, most Justice Department lawyers continue to believe that most agencies, most of the time, are entitled to their day in court and to have the best said in their behalf that the legal imagination can devise—the more so because the agencies are captive clients who cannot seek representation elsewhere.[e]

The divorce also remains intact because, even in the face of the new situation, there are aspects of it that remain positively attractive to both agency lawyers and Justice Department lawyers—at least more attractive than some possible alternatives. While each side sees problems in the way the function of the other is managed, neither would wish to be involved in the other's function more actively than at present if the price of that involvement were the reciprocal involvement of the other side in its function.

There are, after all, several ways to marry the functions, and each side has its *bête noire*, its worst case, the unthinkable thought. For the Justice Department lawyers, there are in fact two "worst alternatives." If the marriage were to entail the wholesale delegation of litigating authority to the operating agencies, not only would Justice lose a large portion of its jurisdiction,[f] but it would also fear for the uniformity of the federal government's litigating position. As I have said, judicial decisions in administrative law tend to ramify, and without the unifying influence of a central litigating agency there is the real possibility that different agencies would advocate conflicting litigating positions, each perhaps affecting adversely

---

[e] Moreover, even where the adversary ideology ends, counseling does not necessarily begin. There is a spectrum of personal views among Justice Department lawyers about agency programs and practices. What one lawyer will find so uncongenial as to be indefensible, another will defend with zeal. In this diversity there are opportunities for skillful management in the assignment of cases, as will be noted by anyone who systematically scrutinizes the recurring names of government counsel who appeared in such controversial litigation as, for example, Selective Service or welfare rights cases.

[f] This is an important consideration, for maintaining both the Department's reputation and the size of its establishment. For example, Social Security litigation—much of which is really quite routine and relatively unimportant—is jealously kept inside the Department, partly because of its volume, which inflates the Department's case load and aids in justifying budget requests, and partly because of the high success rates associated with Social Security cases, which inflates the Department's performance record.

the interest of some other agency. (See Chapter 7 for this and other arguments regarding centralized litigation authority.) If, on the other hand, the Justice Department lawyers themselves were to be dispersed, physically or functionally, among the agencies and their programs, their sense of elitism would suffer. Few Justice lawyers would delight in mastering the cavernous interstices of the Welfare and Pension Plans Disclosure Act or its multiple equivalents in any of a score of agencies. By recruitment, training, and temperament, Justice lawyers take pride in their proximity to the prestige of the courts and their distance from the routine business of their clients. As always, "the image of the judge stands as the image of the lawyer-hero."[34] Now more than ever, there is an irresistible attraction to litigation, for the courts are where the action is.

Agency lawyers, for their part, can well envision a marriage of functions that would entail a diminution of their authority to manage their own business. As the Justice Department lawyers have been given to bemoan what they perceive as the shortsightedness and incapacity of some of their agency counterparts, so the agency lawyers have often found the intervention of Justice lawyers in their affairs to be distasteful, officious, on occasion even patronizing. It is not merely that they, too, wish to preserve their own jurisdiction—though surely they do—but they have sensed correctly that the Justice lawyers commonly have an only imperfect appreciation of the mission, methods, and problems of their agency; and in unusual cases, generally under stress of pending litigation, they have found Justice lawyers downright unsympathetic to their predicament. Of course, the source of this lack of understanding is itself in part the divorce of functions, but it operates to perpetuate the same divorce from which it springs. Moreover, agency lawyers often prefer to have a buffer between themselves and the courts, especially now that the latter have become "unpredictable." In a time of uncertainty, there is considerable intra-agency political utility in having an organization outside the agency responsible for its ups and downs in court.

These, then, are some of the props of the present system. Others will be identified in Chapter 6. To a considerable extent, the old situation is still taken for granted, so that there exists little in the way of counseling to plan for (and avoid) the flow and consequences of litigation or to respond to the spirit of what the courts are trying to convey to the agencies. Both Justice and its clients continue to respond to litigation on a case-by-case basis, avoiding systematic involvement in litigation-oriented counseling by Justice, on the one hand, and program-oriented "education" of Justice by the agency lawyers on the other.

And so the divorce of litigation and counseling is alive, but it is not entirely well. The "new constellation of forces" is making itself felt in subtle ways, and on both sides the lawyers are restless. If each has its worst alternative, each also has some preferred alternatives to the present system. In these alternatives and more generally in the whole process by which the government conducts the bulk of its administrative law litigation, there is more than a little creative, and some not so creative, tension to contend with.

Notes

1. See, e.g., Max Weber, "Bureaucracy," in H.H. Gerth and C. Wright Mills, eds., *From Max Weber* (New York: Oxford University Press, 1958); Chris Argyris, *Understanding Organizational Behavior* (Homewood, Ill.: Dorsey Press, 1960), pp. 12–13; Lewis Gawthorp, *Bureaucratic Behavior in the Executive Branch* (New York: Free Press, 1969), pp. 2–3; Luther Gulick, "Notes on the Theory of Organization," in Gulick and L. Urwick, eds., *Papers on the Science of Administration* (New York: Institute of Public Administration, Columbia University, 1937), pp. 1–45.

2. A concise statement of the apportionment of litigating authority appears in a Department of Justice memorandum: 118 Cong. Rec. 21882-85 (1972).

3. A similar division of labor occurs in some states. For a detailed case study, see Robert Hoag Gordon, "The Relationshup between the Attorney General and Agency Counsels in New York State," Ph.D. thesis, Syracuse University, 1966.

4. 28 U.S.C. § 516. A separate statute (5 U.S.C. § 3106) expressly prohibits heads of departments, unless "authorized by law," from employing attorneys to conduct litigation; it requires them instead to "refer the matter to the Department of Justice." Another (28 U.S.C. § 519) requires the Attorney General (unless otherwise provided by law) to "supervise all litigation to which the United States, an agency, or officer thereof is a party . . . ."

5. For example, 42 U.S.C. § 2035(b) (A.E.C.); 15 U.S.C. § 1508 (Commerce Department); 7 U.S.C. § 2214 (Agriculture Department); 29 U.S.C. § 555 (Labor Department). 31 U.S.C. § 1009, establishing the office of General Counsel of the Treasury Department, contains a disclaimer of any intention to detract from the authority of the Justice Department.

6. The Fair Labor Standards Act permits Labor Department lawyers to appear in litigation, "but all such litigation shall be subject to the direction and control of the Attorney General." 29 U.S.C. § 204(b). A similar provision is contained in the Occupational Health and Safety Act of 1970, 29 U.S.C. § 663. A recent amendment to the Longshoremen and Harbor

Workers' Act goes further, however, by permitting Labor Department lawyers to represent the Secretary of Labor in all courts except the United States Supreme Court. No reference is made to the direction and control of the Attorney General. 33 U.S.C. § 921a. This amendment, passed in 1972, has caused some consternation at the Justice Department.

7. For the lament of a Justice Department lawyer over the specialization he encountered, see Malcolm A. Hoffmann, *Government Lawyer* (New York: Federal Legal Publications, 1956), p. 101.

8. See FTC v. Guignon, 390 F.2d 323 (8th Cir. 1968), in which the Justice Department and the Federal Trade Commission took diametrically opposed positions about the FTC's authority to bring legal proceedings to enforce its own subpoenas.

9. Act of September 24, 1789, ch. 20, § 35, 1 Stat. 92.

10. Act of May 29, 1830, ch. 153. § 5, 4 Stat. 415.

11. See James S. Easby-Smith, *The Department of Justice: Its History and Functions* (Washington: Lowdermilk & Co., 1904).

12. Act of July 2, 1836, § 14, 5 Stat. 82.

13. Act of February 26, 1853, ch. 8, 10 Stat. 161.

14. Act of August 2, 1861, 12 Stat. 285; Act of August 6, 1861, 12 Stat. 327.

15. 1928 ATT'Y GEN. ANN. REP. 344.

16. Act of June 22, 1870, ch. 150, 16 Stat. 162. For the background and consequences of this act, see Homer Cummings and Carl McFarland, *Federal Justice* (New York: Macmillan Co., 1937), chapters 11, 23.

17. CONG. GLOBE, Vol. 91, Pt. 4, 41st Cong., 2d Sess. 3036 (1870) (remarks of Representative Jenckes).

18. Albert Langeluttig, *The Department of Justice of the United States* (Baltimore: Johns Hopkins Press, 1927), pp. 57–60, 190–91.

19. Exec. Order No. 2877 (May 31, 1918).

20. 1928 ATT'Y GEN. ANN. REP. 347.

21. See Cummings and McFarland, *Federal Justice*, pp. 487–89.

22. Exec. Order No. 6166 (June 10, 1933), § 5, in 5 U.S.C. (1964 ed.), p. 159; 5 U. S. C. A. footnote to § 901. The order was upheld and applied in United States v. Paramount Publix Corp., 73 F.2d 103 (C.C.P.A. 1934.)

23. Both history and present practice are described in the Department of Justice memorandum: 118 CONG. REC. 21882-85(1972). Emerging trends are discussed in Chapter 7.

24. For a notable example of this enthusiasm, see James M. Landis, *The Administrative Process* (New Haven: Yale University Press, 1938), chapter 1.

25. 5 U.S.C. §§ 551 *et seq.* In some ways, the new developments were a long-delayed backwash of the APA, which judicialized the procedure of the agencies and made them in many respects just second-class courts. I

have discussed this aspect of the APA in "The Courts as Guardians of the Public Interest," *Public Administration Review*, forthcoming 1977.

26. Administrative Procedure Act, § 10, 5 U.S.C. § 701.

27. See particularly Citizens to Preserve Overton Park v. Volpe, 401 U.S. 402 (1971).

28. See *ibid.* at 415; Conservation Council of North Carolina v. Froehlke, 473 F.2d 664 (4th Cir. 1973).

29. For an extraordinary example of the extent to which this exception has been confined, see Adams v. Richardson, 480 F.2d 1159 (D.C. Cir. 1973) (*en banc*).

30. J. Skelly Wright, *Beyond Discretionary Justice*, 81 YALE L. J. 575–97, 581, 594 (Jan. 1972). See also Environmental Defense Fund v. Ruckelshaus, 439 F.2d 584, 597–98 (D.C. Cir. 1971).

31. 1972 ATT'Y GEN. ANN. REP. 73.

32. "There is little time," reports one former Criminal Division lawyer, "to pause and wonder whether the prisoner [involved in litigation] should be released from prison. It is enough to meet the issues as they are presented by the pleadings and to jump from one case to the next." Hoffmann, *Government Lawyer*, p. 66. To a considerable extent, similar pressures prevail in administrative agency litigation.

33. For a lucid exposition of the adversary system and its assumptions, see Lon L. Fuller, "The Adversary System," in Harold J. Berman, ed., *Talks on American Law* (New York: Vintage Books, 1961), pp. 30–43. See also John Thibaut et al., *Adversary Presentation and Bias in Legal Decisionmaking*, 86 HARV. L. REV. 386–401 (Dec. 1972).

34. David Riesman, "Toward an Anthropological Science of Law and the Legal Profession," *American Journal of Sociology*, Vol. 57 (Sept. 1951), p. 122.

3

The Divorce in Recruitment and Tenure

The divorce of functions is paralleled by a divorce in the recruitment and tenure of government lawyers. This divorce is less complete, but it is still significant. Justice Department lawyers are younger than agency lawyers, they started practicing earlier, they are less experienced and will leave their jobs sooner, and they were recruited from fewer and different law schools.

By and large, the Department of Justice lawyers who handle administrative agency litigation are not career civil servants but birds of passage. Typically, they are recruited fresh from law school. They regard Justice as a desirable place to gain "experience," and so they stay a while and move on to more lucrative or responsible—and more permanent—positions in law firms or, occasionally, other government agencies.

Agency lawyers may also, of course, enter government at the same age and with the same general goals. They, too, may then move on to more attractive opportunities in private or government practice. But they do so with less frequency.

The career patterns of government lawyers fall into positions along a recruitment-tenure spectrum. On several counts, the Justice Department is at one end of that spectrum, while the various agencies are distributed at other points on it. This is clear from data on the composition of three groups of lawyers: the Justice lawyers responsible for the vast bulk of administrative agency litigation (the Civil Division, General Litigation and Appellate Sections), the Office of the General Counsel of the Department of Housing and Urban Development (HUD), and the Office of the General Counsel of the Veterans Administration (VA). There are wide variations among agencies, and so we have selected HUD, a large, active, broad-mission agency with responsibility for major social programs and important new functions added in the last several years, and with considerable power to attract lawyers of some ability, and the VA, an agency with a narrow, relatively stable, mission and rather less drawing power. The differences that emerge, though they are differences of degree, are nonetheless formidable.

Recruitment and Tenure Patterns

As Table 3–1 indicates, the Justice Department lawyers are by far the youngest. Indeed, it is difficult to imagine a younger law office having any

Table 3-1
Distribution of Ages of Government Lawyers
(in percentages)

Age	Justice[a] (n = 41)	HUD[b] (n = 118)	VA[b] (n = 36)
Under 30	42	24	6
30-39	29	27	6
40-49	7	25	16
50-59	7	17	58
Over 59	15	7	14
Total	100	100	100

[a] Civil Division, General Litigation and Appellate Sections only.
[b] Office of the General Counsel only.

Source: *Martindale-Hubbell Law Directory*, Vol. 1, 1971, 1972 (Summit, N.J.: Martindale-Hubbell, Inc., 1971, 1972).

continuity and stability at all. Fully 42 percent of the Justice Department lawyers handling agency litigation are under the age of thirty, and over two-thirds (71 percent) are under forty. Lawyers at HUD are significantly older, though the HUD General Counsel's office can hardly be characterized as senescent. Nearly one-fourth (24 percent) of the HUD lawyers are under thirty, just over half (51 percent) are under forty, and more than three quarters (76 percent) are under fifty. The VA, by contrast, is rather clearly superannuated. Only 6 percent are under thirty, and another 6 percent are under forty, while a cluster of 58 percent falls between fifty and fifty-nine.

The same differences emerge from the median and mean age figures depicted in Table 3–2. One lawyer in seven at Justice is over sixty, and this tends to bring the mean figures for Justice closer to those of HUD and the VA. But the median figures show a spread of nearly a decade between Justice and HUD and an additional decade and a half between HUD and the VA. There may be some younger general counsels' offices than HUD; it is doubtful that any approaches either the youthfulness of Justice or, on the other hand, the maturity of the VA.

A couple of mutually reinforcing factors appear to be at work here. As might be expected of an organization with a rapidly increasing case load— and one dominated by professionals—Justice tends to have a rather "flat" pyramid. For the period represented by these figures, the 41 lawyers in the relevant Justice offices included only 7 with supervisory responsibilities (17 percent); the 118 HUD lawyers included 31 with supervisory duties (26 percent). While salaries at the Department of Justice are favorable, it nevertheless remains true that opportunities for vertical mo-

Table 3-2
Median and Mean Ages of Government Lawyers

	Justice	HUD	VA
Median	30	39	54
Mean	37	40	52

Source: *Martindale-Hubbell Law Directory*, Vol. 1, 1971, 1972

bility are strictly limited by the small number of supervisory positions. Not only are the long-term opportunities at Justice limited by the sparseness of promotion prospects, but the able lawyers who might compete for them are also likely to be tempted by opportunities elsewhere. In many offices at the Department of Justice, including those which handle administrative agency litigation, there is no real expectation that a large number of new lawyers will really spend all or most of their career in the Department.

This is less true at HUD and many other agencies where functional specialization spins off a larger number of smaller offices and new supervisory roles with them. The agency lawyer, if not oriented exclusively to a career within the agency, may at least entertain the prospect of advancement within the agency. The expected result is a higher age structure, as people feel it is in their interest to stay on. That is what the tables reflect.

Moreover, the Justice Department has made a determined effort to attract exactly the kinds of lawyers who are most likely to be career-mobile. Since 1953, the Department has run an extensive Honor Program to recruit outstanding law students when they graduate. Some 50 or more such graduates have been recruited annually under highly competitive conditions. In 1973, when 108 "honor graduates" were hired, there were said to be 2,095 applicants.[1] The hope is that at least some young lawyers who enter the Justice Department in this way can be induced to stay on a career basis, but most do not. Agency general counsels' offices often have similar programs, but they are generally on a smaller scale. The VA has no such program, but HUD does. During each of the last several years, HUD, for instance, has hired approximately ten to twelve lawyers under such a program.[2] Again, therefore, we are dealing with differences of degree, but they are important differences.

The recruiting position of the Department of Justice is enhanced by the nature of its business. The chance to participate in significant litigation in a responsible way is an attractive drawing card for young lawyers. Such opportunities allow recent graduates to use those skills that have been developed most intensively in law school, and they provide a much-sought detour around some of the less interesting work offered to young lawyers by many law firms. In addition, the litigator's ability and training are valued highly by the profession and often presumed to be transferable to other kinds of legal work. Since the agencies do not really conduct their own litigation, they cannot compete with the Justice Department in recruiting on that basis. Yet, some agencies that are charged with the implementation of major social programs, in the civil rights or urban affairs areas, for example, may offset a portion of that disability by the nature of their mission. Nevertheless, litigation would appear to be a magnet that continues to exercise a fairly powerful pull despite vicissitudes of program or leadership.

Some offices within Justice have also undertaken to protect themselves against unduly high turnover by securing commitments to a minimum four-year tenure for prospective legal staff. These commitments are solicited and enforced with varying degrees of strictness and effectiveness.[a] Obviously, commitments of this kind would be quite unnecessary if the lawyers concerned did not have a fair range of outside opportunities to which they might succumb in the absence of a commitment. The attempt to secure commitments thus reflects the existence of alternatives for these lawyers and the desire to limit a natural turnover process.

The agencies typically are not as concerned about minimum tenure as Justice is, because turnover is less of a problem for them. In its recruitment efforts, HUD does attempt to ascertain whether a candidate would at least consider a career in government. An applicant who evinced a clear intention to stay less than two years or had no interest whatever in considering a career at HUD might not be offered a job, but no firm commitment is either sought or obtained by HUD. As we shall see from HUD's tenure statistics, it can afford to be more relaxed than the Justice Department about the length of time a lawyer will spend in the agency.

As the tenure and turnover figures demonstrate, it is not for nothing that Department of Justice officials display anxiety about how long new lawyers will stay with the Department. Ths Justice Department offices handling agency litigation are not only youthful but, on the whole, quite inexperienced. Two-thirds of the Justice lawyers (67 percent) have less than five years' experience; nearly one-third (31 percent) has less than three years' service (Table 3–3). By contrast, the majority (60 percent) of HUD lawyers have more than five years' experience at HUD, and 89 percent of the VA lawyers have been with the VA for more than five years. The median and mean figures set forth in Table 3–4 show the same pattern, although HUD's mean figure is as high as it is (9 years) because of the presence of six people with twenty-five or more years of service.

---

[a] The Tax Division is known to be unyielding about the four-year commitment it extracts; its attitude is something approaching a proprietary interest in its personnel. Other divisions, including the Civil Division, are rather less rigid.

Table 3-3

Duration of Employment of Government Lawyers Employed on December 31, 1970

(in percentages)

Number of Years	Justice (n = 39)	HUD (n = 99)	VA (n = 38)
Less than 1	5	1	0
1-3	26	21	3
3-5	36	19	8
More than 5	33	60	89
	100	101[a]	100

[a]Total does not equal 100 due to rounding.

Source: Departmental records.

Table 3-4

Median and Mean Duration of Employment of Government Lawyers Employed on December 31, 1970

(in number of years)

	Justice (n = 39)	HUD (n = 99)	VA (n = 38)
Median	3	5	18
Mean	5	9	19[a]

[a]This figure is somewhat inflated because, for twelve persons, total federal service, rather than VA service alone, was included. This distortion is not present in the figures in Table 3-3 or the median figures in this table.

Source: Departmental records.

Over time an even more extreme pattern emerges at Justice (Table 3–5). (Unfortunately, comparable figures are not available for the other agencies.) Of 168 lawyers who served at the Department of Justice over a period of six years, more than three-fifths (62 percent) served less than three years, although some did move on to other offices in the Department of Justice. An additional 19 percent stayed from three to five years, and only 18 percent remained on the job more than five years. This suggests that the more limited figures in Table 3–3 are skewed toward the high end of the tenure spectrum, as they might well be, owing to hiring cutbacks in the last several years. In short, government lawyers in general may be *less* experienced than Table 3–3 portrays them; Department of Justice lawyers certainly are.

Table 3-5
Duration of Employment of Department of Justice Lawyers, 1966-72[a]
(n = 168) (in percentages)

Number of Years	Percent
Less than 1	18
1-3	44
3-5	19
More than 5	18
	99[b]

[a] Based on tenure of Justice Department lawyers in the two offices most concerned with agency litigation.
[b] Total does not equal 100 due to rounding.
Source: Departmental records.

Table 3–6 shows that turnover among Justice Department lawyers is also high. In one calendar year, nearly one-third (31 percent) of all the lawyers chiefly responsible for agency litigation left the Civil Division. The HUD and VA figures were lower. More than that, all but one of the VA separations were retirements. The vast majority of Justice departures were resignations. As usual, HUD was in the middle.

It is quite clear from these tables that turnover among Justice lawyers handling agency litigation is inordinately high, that tenure is concomitantly short, and that the two are significantly higher and shorter, respectively, than they are among HUD and VA lawyers.

The age and tenure figures tell us that the Justice Department lawyer is considerably younger than his agency counterpart. They do not tell us something equally significant—that, on the average, the Justice lawyer entered the profession at a younger age than the agency lawyer. As Table 3–7 indicates, the majority of Justice lawyers (61 percent) were twenty-five or younger when they were first admitted to the bar; all but 7 percent of the remainder were under thirty. However, only 39 percent of the HUD lawyers and 28 percent of the VA lawyers were admitted to the bar at age twenty-five or under. Nearly half of both were admitted between the ages of twenty-five and thirty, and one-fourth of the VA lawyers entered their profession at age thirty or older. These late entry figures for the VA, and to a lesser extent for HUD, suggest that many agency lawyers either studied law part time or turned to law school after some other work experience.

A large proportion of VA lawyers (39 percent) studied law in the District of Columbia (Table 3–8). This gives rise to the distinct possibility that many held nonlegal jobs in the federal government before they became

Table 3-6

Turnover of Government Lawyers Based on All Separations During Calendar Year 1971

(in percentages)

Justice (n = 39)	HUD (n = 118)	VA (n = 40)
31	17	20

Source: Departmental figures.

Table 3-7

Age of Government Lawyers at Entry into Legal Profession (First Bar Admission)

(in percentages)

Age	Justice	HUD	VA
Under 26	61	39	28
26-29	32	46	47
Over 29	7	15	25
Total	100	100	100

Source: *Martindale-Hubbell Law Directory*, Vol. 1, 1971, 1972.

Table 3-8

Law Schools Most Commonly Attended by Government Lawyers

(in percentages)

Law School	Justice	HUD	VA
George Washington[a]	5	5	28
Columbia	19	4	0
Harvard	12	4	0
Georgetown[a]	12	8	3
American University[a]	0	2	8
Nebraska	0	1	6
Minnesota	0	1	6
Pennsylvania	5	5	0
Chicago	5	1	0
Virginia	2	3	2
Michigan	2	3	0
Yale	2	2	0
Others	36	61	47
Total	100	100	100

[a] Indicates a law school in Washington, D.C.

Source: *Martindale Hubbell Law Directory*, Vol. 1, 1971, 1972.

lawyers. Whether or not that is the case, the age-of-entry table indicates that many agency lawyers have had considerable employment experience before their professional training was completed—or, in some cases, had even begun. The Justice Department lawyer's job at Justice, however, is almost surely his first full-time position; it is his chance to put to work what he has learned in law school. In his case, but not to the same extent in the case of the agency lawyer, it may be assumed that professional socialization plays a prominent role in guiding behavior.

Large and traditionally better known law schools are more prominently represented at Justice than at HUD or the VA (Table 3–8). Ivy League law schools account for the education of well over a third of the Justice Department lawyers, but of less than half as many HUD lawyers and no VA lawyers. As a matter of fact, the law schools most heavily represented at Justice (Columbia, Harvard, Georgetown) tend to be least heavily represented at the VA, while those most heavily represented at the VA tend to be least heavily represented at Justice (George Washington, American). Once again, HUD is in the middle, in that it draws on schools that feed both Justice and the VA. Interestingly, too, Justice and the VA draw their lawyers from a smaller pool of law schools than does HUD, which tends to have considerable diversity and little concentration in any one school. HUD's largest number of lawyers comes from Georgetown, which provided it with 8 percent, compared to George Washington's 28 percent at the VA and Columbia's 19 percent at Justice.

The schools most represented at Justice are those commonly associated with innovative trends in legal education. Especially since the Justice lawyers generally come there fresh from law school, it is a reasonable surmise that Justice is infused with the skeptical habits of mind generally inculcated at these law schools. Furthermore, graduates of these law schools are in relatively high demand in private practice. This demand reinforces their tendency to move out of Justice once they have completed their apprenticeship in litigation.[3]

Career Patterns and Work Style

The comparative figures on age, tenure, turnover, age of entry into the profession, and law school education provide a rudimentary profile of variations in the career patterns of government lawyers. Some of these variations seem likely to have an impact on style of work.

Short tenure (and high turnover) impedes specialization in agency programs, throws the Justice lawyer back on his generalist skills of reasoning and argumentation, and forces him to rely more on what he has learned in law school and less on what he learns from experience. In all this there is a gap between the Justice lawyer and his agency counterpart, though it is wider for some agencies than others. The agency lawyer is generally steeped in the program with which he has long been associated and expects to continue to be involved. Law school is less relevant to his specialized concerns than his experience is, and he has a longer time to gather the appropriate experience.

These tendencies are reinforced by the heavy flow of litigation at Justice, which pushes the organization toward a necessary fungibility of personnel: Justice lawyers must be "on call" and available to handle whatever litigation seems most pressing, because court-imposed deadlines simply will not wait for a specialist to become available. Thus, the bureaucrat's mastery of a body of specialized information is both impossible, given the Justice lawyer's short tenure, and of limited utility, given the requirements of the case load he must carry. In addition, his education has probably conditioned him to view "excessive" specialization with wariness, if not outright disdain. Finally, the generalism fostered by short tenure and high turnover is quite compatible with the expectations of the courts before which the litigation lawyers appear, as well as with their own way of handling their problems. Judges are, after all, generalists.

Agency lawyers tend to be both older and admitted to the bar at a later age than Justice lawyers. Later recruitment, in particular, may impart to the agency lawyer a somewhat less conventionally "professional" orientation than the Justice lawyer, who is fresh out of law school and working for the first time in a bureaucracy. It is, again, a question of degree and emphasis, of how a government lawyer assigns relative weights to the two roles in which he simultaneously finds himself—lawyer and bureaucrat. A judicial impediment put in the way of "his" program may be taken somewhat more seriously by an agency lawyer than by a Justice lawyer, partly because the agency lawyer is on the scene where the impact is felt, but partly also because his recruitment and tenure probably render him rather more immune to cross-pressuring and susceptible to complete identification with his client. The Justice lawyer, however, tends to be loyal first to his profession, its norms, and its guardians—the judges—and only thereafter to the programs he defends or to his general role as a bureaucrat. In short, he tends to lack a "government view."

Since there is no particular expectation that a Justice lawyer will make his career at Justice (or anywhere else in government), his current position is not an end in itself but a means to some more general career goals. It is, as I have said, his way of gaining "experience." In a measure, this is also true for many agency lawyers, but much less so. The Justice Department lawyer will eventually go out, and he tends to be outward-looking: he takes his cues from the wider professional world beyond the walls of government. His is a threshold work experience; he is less settled in his career than the average agency lawyer, and so more readily adaptable to the rapid changes in judicial doctrine that often offend the sensibilities of agency lawyers.

It would be comforting to conclude, as I have intimated at various points, that the somewhat different recruitment and tenure patterns of Justice and the agencies are congruent with the demands they place on their respective lawyers—that the fit between career lines and role structure is truly complementary. Perhaps there is even a "hidden hand" that allocates to the litigation and counseling functions lawyers whose inclinations are appropriate to those functions. I said it would be comforting to think that this was so, but it would also be misleading. The Department of Justice, for one, is not wholly convinced. Because it wants lower turnover and longer stays in the Department, it extracts minimum commitments, perhaps not fully aware that it has been trading off elite recruitment against longer tenure.

There is a more fundamental reason why a functionalist view of recruitment will not withstand analysis. As judicial oversight of administrative activity increases, it is less and less the case that the litigation lawyers need concern themselves only with the courts while the counseling lawyers focus on the programs of their agencies. Increasingly, the two functions have become intertwined, and what is apt for the old arrangements is not sufficient for the new.

Notes

1. The source of this extremely high figure is the Department of Justice. How serious a candidate each of these applicants was is uncertain, but there is considerable competition for the program.

2. The source for this is the HUD General Counsel's office.

3. As might be expected, all three legal staffs tend also to be drawn heavily from undergraduate colleges and universities in the North and East. The West is almost unrepresented. There are, however, some differences of degree. Including the District of Columbia, the North and East comprise 86 percent of the Justice lawyers, but only 67 percent of the HUD lawyers and 55 percent of the VA lawyers. (The VA has a large component of lawyers who gained their undergraduate degrees in the District of Columbia, and this again may indicate part-time education while working in Washington.) Geographically, Department of Justice lawyers tend to be somewhat more homogeneous and less representative than the other offices. The source of these data is the *Martindale-Hubbell Law Directory, 1971* and *1972*, Vol. 1 (Summit, N.J.: Martindale-Hubbell, 1971, 1972).

4

The Divorce in Practice: The Litigation Process

A prominent effect of dividing legal labor and divorcing legal functions has been to place one set of lawyers in close touch with information about how their agencies operate and another set in close touch with how the courts operate. While some agency lawyers are in charge of preparing for litigation, they are still specialists in the agency's affairs. Some Justice lawyers may regard themselves as specialists in administrative law matters, but their expertise is in the *law* as developed by the courts, rather than the *administration* entrusted to their agency clients. In short, the agencies function at some distance from the courts whose decisions they wish to affect, while the courts are equally removed from the agencies whose behavior they increasingly oversee and seek to modify; each has a separate set of lawyers specializing in its business.

Just how far the courts and agencies are removed from one another is not generally appreciated. In fact, a complex system of communication has been fashioned because of the divorce of functions. It is a system that is stratified both horizontally and vertically, so communications must be passed in stages both upward within each hierarchy and outward from one hierarchy to another. A principal consequence of this network, in turn, has been to keep the litigation lawyers basically ignorant of agency programs, concerns, preferences, and practices, and thus to leave the courts before which these lawyers appear to their own resources in coping with the new burdens of administrative oversight which they have assumed. An equally important consequence has been to insulate the agency lawyers from the pulsebeat of litigation affecting their agencies, and thus to leave their clients, the program managers in the agencies, very much at large in their understanding of what it is that the courts have come increasingly to expect of them, as well as in their ability to predict which of their practices and policies will be sustained and which will not.

In the pages which follow, I shall elaborate these points by tracing the flow of information during the course of litigation. At the same time, we shall have an opportunity to catch a glimpse of the working relations between agency lawyers and Justice Department lawyers at close range, noting the different perspectives they bring to their problems and the impact of these perspectives on the way in which those problems are resolved.

First, however, let me clarify what I mean by "information." One of the threads running prominently through the arguments in favor of judicial restraint has historically involved the limitations presumed to inhere in the character of the judicial process—limitations on data gathering as well as enforcement capacity.[1] If, this argument runs, the courts are to play an active role in national policy making, on what materials will they base their judgments, how will they make their will effective, and how will they know what impact they are having? The "legal realists" of the 1920s and 1930s debunked the "myth of legal certainty," and they questioned the ability of trial judges to establish with reasonable accuracy the "facts" of the lawsuits immediately before them.[2] If this indictment were true of the more or less routine private law business of the courts, how much more would it hold for the far more ambitious adventures of the federal courts into the society, economy, and polity at large or into the administration of the portions of those areas of activity vested in the federal departments and agencies?

Here, then, we are not talking about the concrete "facts" of the cases before the courts, the kinds of facts contained in the documents and testimony that usually constitute the "administrative record" which is placed before the courts for review. These present many of the difficulties that attend judicial "fact finding" in general, as well as some others that derive from the voluminousness of the administrative record on some occasions and its inadequacy on others. The kind of information I have in mind is of a different sort. It is information about the setting of the decision under review, about how the decision fits into the agency's programs, about the sphere of social or economic activity which the agency's action affects, about the rationale and necessity for the authority or the program that is being attacked, about how a decision in one direction or another would pull or tug on a variety of interconnected strings in the agency that are otherwise unseen by the judges. On the other side, we are concerned with the way in which the judicial decisions that emerge return to the agency, how they are read, and whether and how they are integrated into the agency's ongoing programs.

Our focus is thus on the general understanding that the courts have of the agency and the milieu in which it operates and that the agencies have of the judicial mind. If the courts were earlier attempting to shield themselves from deciding in the face of just this kind of ignorance, how are they helped to cope with their ignorance now that their shield has been lowered? And if the agencies were able formerly to manage their own business free from judicial intrusion, how does judicial intervention now get translated into administrative practice?

These are large questions that sensitive lawyers and judges have pondered in various forms for generations. As a practitioner, Brandeis is said to have made a point of knowing more about his client's business than did the client himself, and the celebrated commercial judge Lord Mansfield "used to sit with special juries selected from among experienced merchants and traders. To further his education in commercial practice he used to arrange dinners with his jurors."[3]

To these large questions only very limited answers are available. However, some partial, and not always encouraging, answers flow from the jurocratic communications network as it impinges on the process of judicial review of administrative actions. Let us, therefore, proceed to examine the wiring of that network, beginning with the trial court stage of litigation and then moving on to the appellate stage.

The First-Instance Defense

Once an agency program or action has been challenged by a lawsuit, the general counsel's office undertakes to gather ammunition that will be useful to the Justice Department lawyers in defending the suit. In this the general counsels are of course aided (and often prodded) by those who manage the particular program. Even at this stage, some filtering may occur—both unconscious, because the program managers and agency lawyers are uncertain of precisely what must be revealed to ensure a favorable outcome, and conscious, because advocacy is involved. The important point here is that advocacy is involved in a double sense. The agency naturally wants a victory in court. To obtain this, it must simultaneously convince the Justice Department lawyers and the courts of the merits of the agency action.

At the first stage of most agency litigation—that is to say, in the federal district courts—these are relatively routine exercises. The government wins the vast majority of challenges to agency action in the district courts.[4] Moreover, Justice Department lawyers rarely refuse, as a matter of discretion, to defend challenged agency practices. Several factors are at work.

The first, clearly, is the representative role of the Justice lawyer. It is rather well established that every agency is entitled to be defended at least in the district court, almost irrespective of the nature of the practice that is under attack. Second, this predilection of the Justice lawyers is supported by the government's high success rates in the district courts. Since appeals are expensive for private litigants, there is no assurance that a decision favorable to the government will necessarily be appealed, even if there is some prospect of success for the adverse party on appeal. Third, whereas cost is a factor that private litigants must always contemplate, it is a factor the government almost never contemplates; its lawyers are, so to speak, on permanent retainer. Work load is the closest the government comes to calculating the cost of litigation, but it, paradoxically, is an additional factor pushing the government to defend everything in the first instance. Just as the district courts are overburdened, so are the Department of Justice lawyers who appear before them.[a] To pick and choose among cases to defend and have some assurance that "rational" criteria were being employed in the choice might well be more difficult and time-consuming than simply defending substantially all suits, especially since the refusal to defend would itself have to be defended against the assaults of the agency and its lawyers as they proceeded to "appeal" such a decision, first to the relevant Assistant Attorney General, then to the Solicitor General, and then perhaps even to the Attorney General or the White House. For all these reasons, and also because of the notion that a consistent hard-line defense has a deterrent effect on private litigants, the first-instance defense is routinely and sympathetically accorded the agencies.

The prevalence of favorable outcomes in the district courts does not imply that the district courts are oblivious to the general tendency toward a more prominent judicial role in the administrative process or to what they regard as the failure of many government agencies to discharge their missions appropriately. It is simply that innovation and activism are a bit more likely to come from the appellate courts. Whatever their inclinations, district judges are more constrained by precedent than are appellate judges. Then, too, most district judges conceive their role in terms more limited than the conceptions that prevail in the appellate courts. There are at least three judges sitting on appeal; each of them may reinforce the other's disapproval or incredulity at the way the agency has acted, where one judge might not trust his instincts.[b] Appellate decisions are also effective in a much wider geographic area and stand a far greater chance of becoming "the law of the land" or at least the law of the area or "circuit" over which the court presides. District judges, moreover, are heavily burdened with trial work; they spend a substantial fraction of their working year presiding in court and hearing evidence. Of this burden the appellate courts are relieved; consequently, they are freer to delve more deeply into the validity of agency action, just as they are freer to delve more deeply into most matters that come before them. This, too, tends to make district judges err on the side of caution, for it is much less time-consuming to deny an injunction than to grant one, and they may then take comfort in the possibility of reversal if something "unlawful" has slipped by them.

---

[a] Department of Justice lawyers who appear before district courts are more overburdened than those who handle agency litigation in the appellate courts, though it is difficult to get a precise measure of work load because some cases that are nominally assigned to attorneys in Washington are in fact handled by United States attorneys' offices in the various districts. See note 6.

[b] I appreciate that this proposition about the impact of three-judge panels is more in the realm of plausible hypothesis than revealed truth.

That, after all, is what the appellate courts are for. Activist appellate courts do not, therefore, necessarily breed activist trial courts, at least not one for one.

But if the government tends to receive a sympathetic hearing in the district courts, that is not invariably the case. It is true that the success rates are significantly higher there. Even more, threshold procedural defenses are more likely to keep the district courts from reaching the merits of the challenged agency action; in part this is a result of lag in the diffusion of legal innovation from above. But obviously some district judges are more activist than others, some are more closely attuned to trends in the appellate courts than others, and some are willing to intervene when they sense that the challenged agency action is in some sense unreasonable or unjustified.

To meet this eventuality, the Justice Department lawyer must be prepared to face the merits of the challenged action when and if they arise in the district court. To do this, he will rely heavily on the agency lawyers and what they tell him about the specific action that has been challenged and the broader context in which it is set. Typically, not very much information is passed to Justice at this stage, for several reasons. Not very much is likely to be requested, because the trial lawyers at Justice are, at best, dividing their efforts between the substance of the challenge and the procedural defenses which they hope will win the case (or, in any event, which the trial lawyers want to raise and preserve for a possible appeal). In addition, since there is a little picking and choosing among cases at this level, most cases, save for the obviously serious challenges to agency authority or the occasional *cause célèbre*, are handled in a rather routinized way.[5] Generally, challenges are met by a comprehensive motion for dismissal or summary judgment, often emphasizing jurisdictional and procedural arguments and deemphasizing the importance or complexity of arguments on the merits. Only if that motion fails will the trial lawyer have to confront the difficult issues raised by the complaint. Even then, heavy reliance is apt to be placed on the wording of the statute and regulations and on prior administrative and judicial decisions; resort is often to the ready-made "boiler plate" language resurrected from previous litigation. Correspondingly little weight is generally given to the specific administrative setting and rationale.

If the program has not already become the subject of repeated litigation, or if it is new to the particular lawyer who must defend it, the agency lawyer will undertake to "train" or "educate" his counterpart at Justice in its framework, to the limited extent deemed necessary to the litigation. Still, there is a good bit of slippage between agency and court. If the Justice lawyer is new to the program—a not infrequent possibility, given turnover rates at Justice—he may not appreciate all the ramifications of what he is told. He must, in any case, integrate the defense of this program into the standard defenses used by the government. If the agency has actually drafted a brief, it may or may not be adopted by Justice and filed with the court, depending, among other things, on how well it takes account of the government's general litigating position and how much time is left to start writing from scratch. Work load induces the Justice Department lawyer to file the agency brief more or less as drafted; professional pride impels him to scrap it.

Either way, there may be misunderstandings at the district court stage, as at later stages. In his brief or in oral argument, the Justice lawyer (in many cases, his surrogate, an Assistant United States Attorney[6]) may "say things about the program that are not exactly accurate, or things that have effects elsewhere in the program."[7] What is more, time pressures may force the Justice lawyer to file papers or make representations to the court with less than adequate consultation with the agency lawyers, who are in a position to verify facts and comment on the ramifications of alternative arguments. This naturally leads to frictions. At the district court level, Justice-agency conflicts do not arise as much over litigating position as over litigating procedure. A common complaint of agency lawyers relates to imperfect communications, particularly lack of consultation before the Justice lawyers irrevocably commit the government to a position which may not accord with established agency practice. The net result of the imperfect education of the Justice lawyer and the pressures under which he operates is to limit severely the program information he is able to transmit to the court and render some of it incomplete or misleading.

A difference of "repertoire" may also result in a deemphasis of the particular program in the presentation of the case in court. This may result in something of a dispute over what the government's litigating position ought to be. This possibility is well illustrated by an example from litigation involving housing law. In one lawsuit, an action of the Department of Housing and Urban Development was challenged by local housing authorities on two grounds—one broad and procedural, the other narrow and substantive. The first argument was that HUD had violated the Administrative Procedure Act (APA) by the manner in which it took its action. The second was that HUD had actually exceeded its statutory authority by invading the autonomy of local housing authorities, contrary to a specific statute.[8]

Now the lawyers at HUD were not much concerned with the alleged APA violation, because they could cure it later if it became necessary to do so. But they were very concerned, indeed, about the suggestion that HUD lacked all statutory authority to do what it had done.

Justice, however, had a completely different reaction to the case: the housing-law side of it was *sui generis*, while the APA side of the litigation presented a recurring problem of across-the-board importance to its agency clients. In addition, because of their recurrence, APA questions are grist for the Justice lawyers' mill. Hence there is a readily available fund of experience on which to draw in making APA arguments.

Not surprisingly, Justice argued the APA issue vigorously, but it was far less vigorous and detailed in dealing with the question of HUD's authority. HUD felt obliged to work with certain interest-group interveners in the case, whom it actually aided in presenting the arguments in which HUD was most interested. Even so, the case was lost in the district court, on the issue of HUD's authority. That court did not reach the APA issue. Only on appeal was HUD's authority finally recognized.

In this case, the specifics of the program and the agency's authority were not placed before the court by Justice. It seemed more important and more natural to zero in on the APA questions. Here was a clear-cut case of divergent perspectives flowing directly from the division of labor.

There is another reason for the Justice Department's reluctance to place the substance of the program under attack before the district judge. The inclination of the Justice lawyers is generally not to go to trial, and if too much background information is exposed, there is the danger that the whole subject may be opened up for a full-dress factual hearing. The Department of Justice lawyers, like most defense lawyers, seek to avoid this. If the case can be decided on the "law" alone, the odds are that the agency will prevail; if the case turns on the "facts," the outcome is less predictable. Since money costs are no real factor in government litigation decisions, if it does become necessary to conduct a trial, that can usually be done later, on remand from an appellate court. The prospect of a trial the first time around makes suing the government and its agencies more attractive to potential private litigants, and is therefore to be discouraged. Not only do the Justice trial lawyers share the general defense inclination to avoid a trial, but their additional resources enable them to indulge this inclination somewhat more freely than most private litigants, with highly paid counsel, might be willing or able to do.

On the whole, therefore, relatively little administrative information is transmitted to the federal district courts. Relatively little is demanded. As I have indicated, the agencies might well lose more cases if they did furnish more information at the trial court level. Nevertheless, it does not necessarily follow that it is in the government's interest, even as narrowly conceived in terms of wins and losses, not to furnish more at the district court level. For, time and again, a case easily won in the district court is just as easily lost on appeal. More than that, some arguments received sympathetically in the trial court may get no hearing at all in the appellate court.[9] One of the recurring complaints of Justice appellate lawyers relates to the frequent failure of its trial lawyers to "make a good factual record" in the district court, so as to build a solid case on appeal. (Here the hierarchical division of responsibility within Justice intrudes into the way in which its legal business is managed. It is not the job of the trial lawyers to win cases on appeal, but to win them in the first instance. What may win a case in the district court may lose it on appeal, and vice versa.)

Even at the district court stage, however, it is possible to sense some of the distortions that can occur as information passes from the program managers to the general counsels' offices to the Justice Department trial lawyers and then to the courts. *Not merely are there three stages and four sets of actors involved, but at each stage the recipient of the information is considerably less expert than the conveyer of the information.* At the end of the this process, the judge may have precious little sense for where and how the challenged action fits into the administrative scheme of things, and he may be utterly unable to foresee in what ways and to what extent a decision adverse to the agency will wreak the substantial disruption of the agency's program which the agency inevitably claims it will. Naturally, this uncertainty, though it occasionally gives rise to judicial hostility, tends in general to fortify the judge's inclination to decide the case on procedural grounds or to rule against the challenge on the merits, secure in the knowledge that there are higher courts that may still upset the administrative apple cart if they choose to do so.[10]

There is another distortion that occurs, and it is not attributable to the sparseness of the material made available, to the number of stages through which it passes, or to lack of expertise on the receiving end. This distortion stems from the organizational divorce of functions per se. The fact that litigation involving agency business is handled outside of the agency—by Justice—means that the conduct of the lawsuit is fundamentally outside the control of the agency. If the agency provides too much information on the way it operates, it loses control of that information and creates the risk that it may be misused or misinterpreted or may at some point come back to embarrass the agency. However sympathetic the Justice Department lawyer is, he is a novice in the agency's affairs, and there is no predicting what he may unwittingly but detrimentally reveal in his zeal to win the single lawsuit presently before him. In addition, of course, the agency wants to put on its best face for the lawsuit, so that the Justice lawyer will regard its cause as his and also so that the judge will detect nothing irregular about the agency's proceedings. Advocacy in this double sense cautions against letting any skeletons out of the closet.

The Appellate Stage

Although the agency can almost always count on a vigorous, hard-nosed defense in the district court, it can make no such assumption on appeal. As a matter of fact, it can be stated quite broadly that as the litigation moves up in the judicial hierarchy, from the district court to the court of appeals and then to the Supreme Court, the more adverse become the relations between the agency lawyers and the Justice lawyers. This is a function of two interrelated circumstances. The first is the closer scrutiny that is given to administrative action by the courts on appeal. The second is that the representative role of the Justice Department lawyer declines as the case moves upward. Whereas every agency may be entitled as a captive client to one defense, it is not automatically assumed that it is necessarily entitled to be defended all the way to the Supreme Court.

These two factors are interrelated, because the closer scrutiny given to agency action by the appellate courts forces the appellate lawyers at Justice to take a closer look at the challenged agency action with a view to forecasting whether and how it can be sustained on appeal. Not only are they concerned about the possibility of losing a given case, but they must also worry about the potential impact of a loss on all their other cases. If they lose a given case, they may also lose in the process a rule of law favorable to the government across the board, and, by arguing vigorously for a position the courts regard as untenable, they may simultaneously diminish their credibility with the courts in future cases. Hence, Justice Department lawyers worry about the consistency of the positions they take. "Unfortunately," states one memorandum urging the Solicitor General to decline to authorize an appeal requested by the affected agency, "we have lost meritorious cases because our perceived willingness to take inconsistent positions diminishes courts' confidence in our integrity and prejudices their receptivity to our arguments." Because an inconsistent position had been taken in an earlier suit, no appeal was taken in this one, even though both positions were regarded as being about equally meritorious.[11] While the agency lawyers are concerned with one piece of litigation and one program at a time, the Justice lawyers are watchful of the effect of any single lawsuit on the whole run of their litigation, both pending and future.

This point needs to be underscored, because it lies at the heart of many of the conflicts over litigating position that arise between the Justice Department and the agencies at the appellate level. Because Justice is the barrister for all the agencies, it cannot allow the interests of one to overshadow or damage the interests of all. And because Justice is constantly in court, it must worry about the esteem in which it is held by the judiciary, for that esteem is presumed to have an impact on success rates in general. Justice tends to believe that if it indiscriminately defends the indefensible, a boy-who-cried-wolf effect may set in with the courts, and that such an effect would in all probability be counterproductive. Indeed, Justice lawyers are likely to attribute, probably with some accuracy, the demise of the procedural roles that earlier protected the agencies from judicial intervention to precisely the sort of indiscriminate across-the-board defense of agency action that the agencies are constantly urging Justice to undertake.

There is some reluctance to assert blanket defense in cases that might be lost if the courts were to pierce those defenses and reach the merits. The fear is that, if the cases are unattractive, the courts will begin to whittle away at the blanket defenses in general, which would impair their overall utility. When Selective Service litigation was commonplace during the Vietnam war, litigation lawyers began to think twice before asserting the statutory bar to preinduction judicial review of draft board orders where the board's action seemed unusually arbitrary; they were chastened by the government's experience with that defense.[12] By the same token, the Justice Department lawyer may be a bit wary of invoking the "discretionary function" exception to the Federal Tort Claims Act[13] where the negligence of the agency involved is plain enough for all to see, for fear that the courts, in their urge to see justice done, will gradually obliterate the exception by rendering fewer and fewer functions "discretionary." Slowly the same position began to be reached with common use of executive privilege to thwart disclosure of documents under the Freedom of Information Act.[14] As the courts grew skeptical, Justice began to lose its enthusiasm for routine claims of privilege.

The agencies tend to compute their cost-benefit ratio rather differently. For them, the case at hand is of principal importance. Winning it is the goal. In each such case, the agency must bear only a small increment of the total loss of credibility that may arise from repeated invocation of blanket defenses, and just such a defense might win that particular case. The heightened importance of the particular case, the diminished importance of government cases in general, and the agencies' greater distance from judicial reactions all lead the general counsels' offices to a less discriminating attitude toward the defenses to be employed than is found at Justice.

Deciding to Appeal

There is, therefore, some pulling and tugging between the general counsels' offices and Justice at the appellate level as the representative role recedes somewhat and the Justice lawyers agonize over whether and on what grounds the case can be won on appeal. There are, of course, two general postures in which the case can reach the appellate stage: the agency has either lost or won in the district court. Two different courses follow from these two different outcomes. I deal with them in order.

If the government has lost in the district court (or, for that matter, in the court of appeals), there is no presumption that it will take an appeal (or petition for certiorari). Indeed, a substantial majority of the government's losses in the district courts and the courts of appeals are not appealed to the next stage.[15] Some of these losses are not appealed for the obvious reason that the probability of success on appeal is judged to be slight. Some such cases, however, are simply judged to be of no general importance to the agency or the government. Others may involve an especially important point for the agency or the government, but they may have arisen in so unappealing a factual context as to evoke the reaction that they are not the "right case" on which to risk an important legal point; or they may be the right case but in the "wrong court"—that is, a court already on record as being opposed to the government's position. Still other cases may not be appealed because the claim of the adverse party is judged to have equitable though not legal merit, so that only the most heartless or narrowly legalistic judge could find it in his conscience to ignore the factual background in favor of adherence to strict legal doctrine. This last possibility occurs with considerable frequency in Social Security disability cases.

The decision to appeal is an entirely discretionary one confided in the final instance to the Solicitor General.[16] More than that, the decision to appeal can itself be regarded as a quasi-judicial determination often made in an adversary framework. In each case, the recommendations of the affected agency or agencies are routinely sought, and the decision of the Solicitor General or his deputy is based on these recommendations and the recommendations prepared by the Justice lawyers.

Will the agency and Justice recommendations agree? Obviously, there are four possibilities, only three of which occur with any degree of frequency. First, the agency may recommend against appeal, while Justice may recommend in favor. This is a rare occurrence, because Justice is concerned about the impact of an appeal on the government's litigating position in general and hence recommends fewer appeals than the agencies, because Justice is likely to defer to a no-appeal recommendation by the client agency affected by the loss, and because cases in which the agency is not at least nominally in favor of appeal are not likely to be very meritorious cases from the government's standpoint. The second (more probable) possibility is that Justice and the agency agree that an appeal is warranted. The adverse decision may be so overwhelmingly "in error" that the need for rectification is manifest to all. The third possibility is that both sides recommend against appeal. This is likely where the case is unimportant, the judge's reasoning is persuasive, or the agency is willing to rest after its day in court.

A moment ago, I called the process of deciding whether to appeal an adversary process. The fourth possibility is really what makes it that. The agency may favor an appeal, while the Justice lawyers argue against it.

This is not an infrequent occurrence; the general counsels' offices are urged to fight for the agency's programs by the program managers, and it is often preferable to have Justice assume the unpleasant responsibility for throwing in the towel. Organizational separateness thus makes Justice a convenient scapegoat for decisions which, if made intramurally, might impair the continuing confidence reposed by the departmental staffs in their legal offices. The general counsels also fear that, if they accept a loss, they will invite further judicial intrusions into their business, or that, if they acquiesce in a recommendation against appeal, Justice will (as it sometimes has) use the acquiescence as a precedent against the agency in future cases. The agency lawyers are thus impelled toward appealing a wider range of cases than the Justice lawyers, who entertain the rather different perspective that has been described.

The four possible outcomes are illustrated in Table 4-1 for a sample of 374 cases lost in the district court. The table compares agency appeal recommendations with Justice Department appeal recommendations.[17] It includes all cases that reached the desks of six appellate attorneys during their stay in the Department of Justice. The only exceptions are cases in which there were no agency recommendations, principally cases arising under the Federal Tort Claims Act. Included is a large number of Social Security cases which usually (especially in the disability area) raise only factual, hence generally unappealable, issues. In a moment we shall see what the omission of these cases does to the table.

To what extent are the Justice lawyers' recommendations a function of differences in the kinds of cases assigned to particular attorneys or of the attorneys' own inclinations to recommend appeals? There may be, of course, a differentiation of styles. Some Justice lawyers may take their screening role somewhat more seriously than others and disagree with agency recommendations more readily. Some, on the other hand, may take their representative role more seriously, deferring to the wishes of their agency clients even in cases where, as an original matter, they might have arrived at a different recommendation. In view of the room for individual variations in work style, it is striking how similar the cells look when the work of one attorney is compared to that of another, as it is in Table 4-2. The table is arranged so that the figures for each attorney appear in the same position in each cell.

The consistencies here are extraordinary, and bespeak a greater homogeneity of role orientation than might have been expected, given individual differences in assignment, ability, and viewpoint. With the exception of one attorney who disagrees with agency appeal recommendations more rarely than anyone else (which, I think, suggests not a personal idiosyncrasy, but assignment to him of a disproportionate number of obvious no-appeal cases), the rank-ordering of cells in the table is the same for

Table 4-1
Appeal Recommendations in 374 Administrative Agency Cases Lost by the Government in Federal District Court, 1966-73
(in percentages)

Agency Recommendation	Justice Recommendation		
	Appeal	*No Appeal*	*Total*
Appeal	26	9	35
No Appeal	0.5	64	65
Total	27	73	100

Table 4-2
Appeal Recommendations in 374 Administrative Agency Cases Lost by the Government in Federal District Court, 1966-73 (By Individual Attorneys)
(in percentages)

Agency Recommendation	Justice Recommendation		
	Appeal	*No Appeal*	*Totals*
Appeal	34	20	54
	26	10	36
	26	10	36
	26	4	30
	25	14	39
	23	1	24
No Appeal	0	46	46
	0	64	64
	1	62	63
	0	70	70
	0	62	62
	1	75	76
Totals	34	66	100
	26	74	100
	27	72	99[a]
	26	74	100
	25	76	101[a]
	24	76	100

Assuming randomness in assignment of cases, $X^2 = 38.63$; $p < 0.001$.
[a] Total does not equal 100 due to rounding.

each attorney. The largest fraction of cases is in the agency no-appeal-Justice no-appeal cell; next is agency appeal-Justice appeal, then agency appeal-Justice no-appeal, and in last place agency no-appeal-Justice appeal. For each attorney, agreement with the agencies heavily outweighs disagreement. Furthermore, every attorney recommends against appeal more frequently than he recommends in favor of appeal, and the total range of variation from attorney to attorney is only 10 percentage points. This, despite the fact that there is considerable variation in agency recommendations, which I believe reflects differences in cases assigned to the attorneys, as well as differences in individual skills in persuading agencies to "get in line." Agency pro-appeal recommendations vary by Justice Department attorney as much as 30 points, from a low of 24 percent to a high of 54 percent—in other words, a range of variation three times as great as the range of variation in the Justice attorneys' own recommendations.

So obviously significant is the number of Social Security benefit cases and so differential is their impact on the various cells that it is worth looking at appeal recommendations with the Social Security benefit cases omitted. When we do this, in Table 4-3, the rank-ordering of the four cells by number of cases stays constant, but there is a considerable drop in the percentage of unanimous no-appeals (from 64 to 41) and a slightly less pronounced but still significant rise in the fraction of unanimous pro-appeals (from 26 to 40 percent). Justice Department dissent from agency no-appeal recommendations remains virtually nil, but disagreements between Justice and the agencies, when the latter have recommended in favor of appeal, double (from 9 to 18 percent). Being disproportionately routine, the Social Security litigation masks the extent of disagreement between Justice and the agencies, for the two fail to compose their differences about one-fifth of the time and they start out disagreeing much more frequently than that.

With the Social Security cases removed, agency appeal recommendations continue to show great variation from attorney to attorney (Table 4-4). But every Justice Department attorney except one continues to recommend against appeal more frequently than in favor, though the range of variation from attorney to attorney increases from 10 to 20 percentage points (Tables 4-2, 4-4). This reflects again the fact that Social Security benefit cases are more routine than others, and there is strong consensus on how to handle them. There is plainly more variation possible in assignments in the general run of agency litigation than in Social Security cases.

However, Table 4-4 also shows that there is some diversity of operating style among attorneys. When one lawyer disagrees with agency pro-appeal recommendations in only 3 percent of all his cases while having the largest fraction of unanimous no-appeals (57 percent), whereas other lawyers disagree with the agency in one-fourth of all their cases without being "appeal-shy," it seems obvious that some Justice lawyers take their representative function more seriously than their screening function, and vice versa. Again, though, it is probably true that the composition of his

Table 4-3
Appeal Recommendations in 194 Administrative Agency Cases Lost by the Government in Federal District Court, 1966-73 (Excluding Social Security Benefit Cases)
(in percentages)

Agency Recommendation	Justice Recommendation		
	Appeal	No Appeal	Total
Appeal	40	18	58
No Appeal	1	41	42
Total	41	59	100

Table 4-4
Appeal Recommendations in 194 Administrative Agency Cases Lost by the Government in Federal District Court, 1966-73 (Excluding Social Security Benefit Cases, By Individual Attorneys)
(in percentages)

Agency Recommendation	Justice Recommendation		
	Appeal	No Appeal	Totals
Appeal	56	17	73
	48	24	72
	42	25	67
	37	3	40
	35	26	61
	33	15	48
No Appeal	0	28	28
	0	29	29
	0	33	33
	3	57	60
	0	39	39
	2	50	52
Totals	56	45	101[a]
	48	53	101[a]
	42	58	100
	40	60	100
	35	65	100
	35	65	100

Assuming randomness in assignment of cases, $X^2 = 70.99$; $p < 0.001$.
[a] Total does not equal 100 due to rounding.

case load deviated somewhat from the norm. But with the Social Security benefit cases removed, the absolute numbers of cases for each lawyer are small, and therefore not too much can safely be inferred from individual variations.

Returning to the aggregate figures, it is interesting to see in Table 4-3 *how few cases Justice is inclined to appeal (41 percent) and how much more frequently the agencies recommend appeal (58 percent). In 18 percent of all cases excluding Social Security benefit cases, the affected agency has recommended appeal, but the Department of Justice lawyers have recommended against appeal.* Given the representative role of the advocate and the many ways of avoiding disagreement (to be described shortly), this is a significant incidence of intragovernmental conflict.

The conflict results from differing premises. As I have said, Justice begins with no presumption that an adverse decision will be appealed. The agency lawyers tend to approach their cases with the opposite presumption. As a lawyer for a department with a good deal of litigation described his position: "I presume that I am going to recommend that we go for appeal unless what the district court has done is totally inconsequential. If the case only involves a few dollars, then we won't go up, but otherwise we want an appeal."[18]

Curiously, it is the *agencies* that are reluctant to abandon a case on grounds of prudence, policy, or cost if there is any reason whatever to think that the court has made an error of law. This is true despite the fact that, in principle at least, administrative agencies are supposed to respond flexibly to extralegal "administrative" considerations. On the other hand, Justice—a department of lawyers and only lawyers—is prone to base its recommendation on the factual setting of the particular case, the frequency with which the underlying problem recurs, its estimated importance (or lack of importance) to the agency or the government as a whole, and similar considerations going beyond the question of whether the court below was "in error." It should be said, however, that these proclivities of Justice lawyers derive less from a sense of the appropriate role of the agency client than from experience with how the courts are likely to respond to certain kinds of cases and the perceived need to represent the interest of all the agencies, not merely the one now before the court.

In view of the fact that Justice recommends against appeal in a substantial minority of cases where the agencies recommend in favor (18 percent), it is interesting that Justice almost never recommends in favor of appeal where the agencies do not (1 percent) (Table 4-3). The prevailing conception is that the agency is the client, and it determines what losses it can accept. The difference is between action and inaction: the lawyer, it is believed, may not have to do everything his client asks, but if the client *asks nothing*, the lawyer should *do nothing*. If, therefore, the agency wants to abandon the cause, its wishes should be respected.

The very few exceptions to this pattern of deference occur where a legal principle of applicability to several agencies is at stake. That principle may be of little significance to the agency recommending against appeal, but it may affect the business of other agencies more seriously—so seriously that the Justice lawyers may actually be on the lookout for a good case to take up on appeal, as, for example, they were at one time in the lien priority area. The government's lien priorities, provided by statute, are important because they confer on the government as creditor a special position with respect to property that is often insufficient to satisfy all the claims on it. Since a number of agencies may hold priority liens, this is a subject that cuts across departmental lines, and an adverse decision may redound to the disadvantage of several agencies. One appealing lien priority case did eventually come along. While it was trivial to the agency that lost it, the ramifications of the decision were considerable, and the case itself was an attractive one to take to an appellate court—"a beauty," as a Justice Department lawyer described it. Since the facts presented the legal issue in a favorable setting, Justice recommended that the case be used as a vehicle to make the general argument for the government's lien priority position, despite the agency's contrary recommendation.

This, of course, is a departure from the usual norms of attorney-client relations. It is not surprising that there are few such cases. The 1 percent figure in Table 4-3 includes only two cases; in both, the Justice argument was a general one that would apply across agencies. One involved the award of interest and attorneys' fees; the other, the court's jurisdiction over the subject matter. In the former, the issue had not been raised by the government in the district court; in the latter, the court had not considered the issue, so it could hardly be said to be a damaging precedent against the government. In neither case did Justice really pursue the pro-appeal recommendation wholeheartedly.

If Justice insists on taking an appeal in the face of a contrary recommendation from the affected agency, the agency is likely to regard it more or less as a matter of indifference. After all, the Justice Department, not the agency, will assume the burden of pursuing the appeal, and its action will probably not hurt the agency in any way. Conceivably, agency lawyers may even be fired with a new enthusiasm for the cause when they learn of Justice's unusual zeal to pursue the matter. It is not uncommon to find an agency altering its recommendation from no-appeal to pro-appeal once it learns that Justice is disposed to recommend in favor of appeal. This accounts for the very few cases in the lower-left cell in Table 4-3.

Important as it is to highlight the two cells of Table 4-3 that indicate agency-Justice disagreement, it is also important to stress that the two sets of recommendations converge in some 81 percent of the cases—although we shall see that this figure sometimes reflects nominal rather than genuine agreement. What is more striking is that *both Justice and the agencies recommend against appeal in an exceptionally large proportion of cases: 41 percent* (64 percent if Social Security benefit cases are included). Given the fact that the government has a stable of litigation lawyers on what is essentially permanent retainer and that it makes no calculation of money costs in its litigation decisions, this is a large fraction of cases in which the agencies and Justice have jointly determined that it is wiser to accept defeat in the district court than pursue an appeal. The figure is even more exceptional when it is considered that the total number of cases includes a few suits filed by the government as plaintiff; in these cases, advance consideration was presumably given to the agency's litigating position, and losses would less readily be accepted by the agency without appeal.

As I have said, there is an important respect in which these figures are misleading. They represent only formal recommendations, and for this reason they understate the extent of the differences between Justice and the agencies. Because the percentages represent the aggregate of tactical decisions made by parties in continuing relationships with one another, they do not necessarily reflect the views that each genuinely entertains about his cases. There are a number of techniques employed on occasion to minimize the incidence of conflict between sets of recommendations and to reduce the potential for unfavorable outcomes in bureaucratic battles. The high rates of agreement thus conceal important differences of approach.

First, it is possible for the Justice lawyer, faced with an agency recommendation favoring appeal, to endorse that recommendation in form but not really in substance. He may state that his recommendation accords with the agency recommendation, while at the same time pointing out to the Solicitor General's office in the course of his memorandum (or perhaps on the phone) all the weak spots in the agency's case. This Aesopian language purporting to favor an appeal in what is made to look like an unappealing case is generally understood to be the weak endorsement that it is, and it generally produces a negative decision. (In such cases, the Solicitor General may take approximately the same tack, expressing his agreement with the agency's position in principle but his reluctance to appeal until he has a "better case" with which to make the legal argument.) The risk of writing a weak memorandum purporting to endorse the agency's position is that the "no appeal" signals that it is intended to convey may be misread in the Solicitor General's office or that a lawyer in that office who sees the case differently will be able to indulge his views without fear of precipitating a clash with the Civil Division lawyer. In either event an appeal authorization may be unintentionally triggered. But the frequency and success with which the well-known "no-appeal appeal memorandum'' is employed is indicated by the fact that several Justice Department lawyers spontaneously reminded me of the practice in order to caution against drawing hard-and-fast conclusions from the bare figures.

Second, to avoid an unpleasant conflict or to manipulate the outcome, the Justice lawyer may persuade his agency counterpart of the futility of recommending an appeal that stands no real chance of being authorized by the Solicitor General. If he follows this course, the Justice lawyer is trading on the general counsel's experience with previous appeal recommendations that were unsuccessful in the Solicitor General's office, together with his only imperfect predictive knowledge of exactly what moves the Solicitor General to decide one way or the other. The gratuitous advice to the agency for it to recommend against appeal thus sometimes contains the elements of bluff, yet it occasionally succeeds. To preserve his credit at Justice and/or to avoid a conflict with at best a chancy outcome, the general counsel may capitulate earlier rather than (as he has been led to believe) later, and recommend against appeal. Sometimes, of course, he may yield only after a fight, but the low rates of agency success in the Solicitor General's office have generally resulted in a change of venue, so that many such battles are now fought in the office of the Assistant Attorney General for the Civil Division. Where they produce a change of agency recommendation, these disagreements are not reflected in Tables 4-1 through 4-4.

Third—and less deviously—either side may independently see what it regards as the handwriting on the wall and tailor its recommendations accordingly. Given its experience with the Solicitor General's niggardliness in pursuing appeals from adverse decisions, the agency may recommend against appeal despite its conviction that an appeal is warranted. For its part, Justice may bow to the agency's unflinching determination to fight what Justice sees as a hopeless case, and recommend in favor of appeal, notwithstanding its inclination to the contrary. Whatever its convictions, either side may base its recommendation on a prediction of the probable outcome of a disagreement, should one come to pass.

As these techniques—and the representative role, which impels the advocate to defer to his client's wishes—suggest, there is the possibility that, even in cases where they formally agree, both sides entertain quite different views of the litigation. The conclusion that agency and Justice appeal recommendations agree in 81 percent of the decisions they lose in the district courts cannot, therefore, be accepted without substantial qualification. Genuine agreement is much less frequent.

Since the decision to appeal a loss is explicitly made from scratch, on the basis of potentially competing recommendations, the participants are caught in a process of advocacy within a process of advocacy. The same lawyer who will be called upon to prosecute the appeal, if it is authorized, may be, for the moment at least, marshalling his evidence and arguments against the position of the agency he will have to urge on the appellate court if he loses before the Solicitor General. Temporarily, therefore, and again if there is a subsequent appeal decision to be made, the Justice lawyer cannot be viewed as sitting entirely on the same side of the table as the agency lawyer.

All this bears, and bears heavily, on the flow of administrative information from the agency to Justice. At this stage, that flow is impeded not only by the general loss of control over information once released, but by the process of advocacy that is occurring.

The contest is, to begin with, not entirely even: the Justice recommendations more frequently prevail with the Solicitor General, who, like the Justice lawyers—only more so—is worried about the government's general litigating position and its credibility with the courts. Table 4–5 shows that Justice wins all but a small number of disagreements between it and the agencies over whether an appeal is warranted. The table sets forth the rates of authorization of appeals by the Solicitor General according to the recommendations of the Department of Justice and the affected agencies. Where both recommended appeal, the Solicitor General authorized appeal in 94 percent of the cases. He never authorized appeal where both recommended against appeal or in the two cases where the agency recommended against but Justice recommended in favor, and he authorized appeal in only 9 percent of all the cases in which the agency favored appeal but Justice opposed it.

It is obvious from the table that the Solicitor General's office relies heavily on agency and Justice recommendations in deciding whether to authorize appeal.[19] Unanimous recommendations are followed in nearly all cases, and in literally all cases in our sample where the unanimous recommendation was *against* appeal. Justice recommendations favoring appeal are followed more frequently than those of the agencies (92 percent to 71 percent). This, of course, is another way of saying that the Solicitor General authorizes relatively few appeals: 25 percent.[20] This figure should be compared to the percentages of Justice and agency pro-appeal recommendations: 27 and 35 percent, respectively (Table 4-5).

Although Justice Department recommendations carry more weight than the agencies', it remains true that, if *either* recommends against appeal, the chances that an appeal will be authorized are extremely slim. In the few cases where an agency pro-appeal recommendation has prevailed over a Justice no-appeal recommendation, the Solicitor General or his deputy may have discerned an important principle at stake in the case that had been neglected or placed at a lower level of priority by Justice; or else someone at Justice formally recommending against appeal may informally

Table 4-5

Cases in which the Solicitor General Authorized Appeal in 374 Administrative Agency Cases Lost by the Government in Federal District Court, 1966-73 (By Agency and Justice Department Recommendations)
(all figures in percentages)

Agency Recommendation	Justice Recommendation		
	Appeal	*No Appeal*	*Total*
Appeal	26	9	35
Of these the Solicitor General authorizes:	94	9	71
No Appeal	0.5	64	65
Of these the Solicitor General authorizes:	0	0	0
Total	27	73	100
Of these the Solicitor General authorizes:	92	1	25

Figures above the dotted lines reflect the Justice Department and agency recommendations as a percentage of all cases, as in Table 4-1. Figures below the dotted lines reflect the Solicitor General's authorization of appeal *as a percentage of the cases in that cell above the dotted line.*

have been urging the opposite course; or the Solicitor General may deliberately have been making a concession to an agency whose wishes he had recently thwarted in some other litigation. Examples of each of these possibilities are to be found in the cases that form the basis of the table.

In 6 percent of the cases where agency and Justice lawyers both recommended in favor of appeal, the Solicitor General declined to authorize one. In some, the Justice recommendation was only nominally affirmative: it was the "no-appeal appeal recommendation" described above. The other cases in which the Solicitor General overruled unanimous pro-appeal recommendations fall into one or more of several relatively clear-cut categories. The decision to be appealed may have been a very limited one that applied only to the peculiar factual situation in that case and one, therefore, of no general importance to the government. Alternatively, while the legal case may have been strong, "the facts" may have been weak or there may have been another stronger case available to take up on appeal to make the same point; or the legal case may simply have been weak, and even the agency may not have been strongly urging that an appeal be taken. Lastly, there may have been a procedural problem with the case; for example, there may have been some legal question about the appealability of the district court order in question. All these circumstances may be found in the cases that comprise the 6 percent in which the Solicitor General refused to permit an appeal recommended by Justice as well as the agency concerned.

This residual category demonstrates graphically that the Solicitor General retains a strategic and tactical—in a word, prudential—as well as purely legal veto over appeal authorizations. As we have seen, he is inclined to appeal fewer cases than the Justice lawyers who make their recommendations to him, and, *a fortiori*, he is at odds with the agencies even more often. Like the Justice lawyers, but more so, he differs with the agencies not so much on the legal merits of their cases as on the wisdom and expediency of pursuing them to their outermost limit.

Table 4-5 accords well with data derived from other sources. In a dissertation on the Solicitor General's office, William Edward Brigman has analyzed 9789 decisions regarding appeal to the courts of appeal over the ten-year period from 1952 to 1961. Brigman finds that appeals to the court of appeals are authorized in 27.5 percent of all losses and 21.0 percent of all Civil Division losses.[21] These figures are very close to those presented above, for it should be remembered that I have omitted cases in which there was no agency recommendation, and those are disproportionately on the no-appeal side. Brigman also finds that certiorari is authorized in 11.0 percent of all possible certiorari cases.[22] This figure does not quite have an equivalent in our Supreme Court certiorari and appeal data. But, despite the differences in the composition of the pool of cases, the results were the same: certiorari was authorized in 10.5 percent of all the agency cases in the work of the Justice attorneys surveyed.

Brigman has disaggregated his figures by agency as well. Though the number of cases from any one agency is generally too small to permit firm inference, it appears that the agencies vary widely by (1) the fraction of their losses that are appealed, (2) the frequency with which they recommend appeal, and (3) the frequency with which their pro-appeal recommendations are heeded.[23] Some agencies are more persuasive than others, some are more careful in preparing appeal recommendations, and some, by the grace of Congress, are simply endowed with a stronger legal position than others. As is to be expected, all the agencies have less success with their pro-certiorari recommendations than with their pro-appeal recommendations; fewer cases are authorized by the Solicitor General for Supreme Court review.[24]

Despite variations from agency to agency, it remains true that Justice retains the upper hand in disputes with agencies over whether to take an appeal. The agencies are parties aggrieved by their losses; they are likely to seek vindication through appeal. Justice, on the other hand, can afford the luxury of the independence that is always conferred on bystanders.

That Justice prevails in nearly all cases of formal disagreement with the agency does not mean that the same outcomes would be reached if agency recommendations were dispensed with altogether. As we have seen, there is a certain amount of mutual adjustment that may occur before the formal agency and Justice recommendations emerge: the proportion of appeals recommended by each would be quite different without the recommendations of the other.

Likewise, the fact that Justice often prevails after conferences over disputed recommendations have been held in the Solicitor General's office does not mean that agency lawyers are wasting their time requesting such conferences. To be sure, the manifest purpose of the conference—to persuade the Solicitor General to authorize an appeal—is rarely achieved. Yet there may be latent purposes, too.

By going over to the Department of Justice, the agency general counsel may convince his clients in the agency that he has truly gone to the barricades for them but met a Goliath too stubborn to see the merit of the agency's position. Not a few such conferences, ostensibly convoked for combat, have been consumed in an exchange of pleasantries and witticisms. It is often not what he *did* there, but that he *went* there, that ingratiates the general counsel with the agency staff.

Again, the agency lawyers may have another purpose in mind. They may sense that persuasion and cajolery may not avail in *this* case, and so they may seek to extract a commitment that, in the *next* case, provided the "facts are right," the Solicitor General will fight to the end. Such promises are probably almost as often given as sought if the grounds for not appealing do indeed relate to the factual setting of the case or the limited nature of the holding of the court below, or some other such characteristic that may not be present in future cases.

If such a promise is the agency lawyer's objective, what he is actually seeking is a determination that the Solicitor General's opinion has only limited value as a precedent. Occasionally, the pattern of appeal decisions does suggest that an appeal may be authorized simply to placate an adamant general counsel, unhappy about having lost too often in the Solicitor General's office.[25] But this result is achieved by repeatedly carrying disputes to the Solicitor General's office, rather than by limiting the precedential value of the Solicitor General's decision. A decision read narrowly today may be read expansively tomorrow, and it is far easier to extract a promise to appeal the next such case than it is to enforce it.

Stubbornness as a strategem may also have utility outside the Solicitor General's office. If the client exudes enough of it, the lawyer may find the encounters distasteful enough to induce him to yield when he can. An agency with a reputation for fighting over every case of disagreement may thus be able to extract concessions more readily than a cooperative agency that has regularly recognized the wisdom that resides in the Department of Justice. Aggressive clients, as the Labor Department sometimes is, generally are handled with somewhat greater care by Justice (to avoid a fight) than are diffident clients.

Finally, the general counsel may seek to use the conference for a more immediate purpose: to obtain an authoritative interpretation of the judicial opinion in question for the operations of their agency. The agency lawyers have probably been asked *their* opinion of what the court's ruling means, and they may want to be sure that it does not mean what some in the agency may fear it means.

Lest there be any doubt on this score, the interpretation they seek from the Solicitor General is the narrowest one possible, and the chances are good that at least their worst fears will be allayed. One of the arguments most emphasized in Justice recommendations against appeal is that the decision below does not affect the interests of the agency in the sweeping way that the agency may have believed. This view will probably be conveyed in some form to the anxious agency lawyers, who may then advise the affected offices in the agency that they can continue to do (or not do) most of what they have previously been doing (or not doing). Some hard-fought agency-Justice conferences have ended this way. It should be noted, however, that if the Solicitor General provides an off-the-cuff legal opinion of this kind, he does so, typically, with little knowledge of the agency's operations. That, however, may not prevent the agency from relying on this opinion, for agency lawyers often express considerable deference to the judgment of the Solicitor General.

The appeal or certiorari conference in the Solicitor General's office, though it rarely changes the minds of the participants, may still serve a purpose, albeit not to decide whether an appeal is warranted. What seems like pointless ritual—and doubtless is from the standpoint of the Solicitor General—may prove to be a useful exercise for the agency lawyers from several vantage points.

Deciding whether to take an appeal is, as I have said, an adversary process. Like any advocate, the agency lawyer is engaged in an enterprise at once predictive and persuasive. As a sender of information, he seeks a favorable result based on that information. Consequently, the general counsels' offices provide reasons for appeal or for the rule of law they favor—reasons they believe will be palatable to the Justice lawyers, the Solicitor General's office, and the courts. In this criterion, there are two separate sources of distortion.

In the first place, the agency lawyers and the program managers on whom they in turn rely for their information screen out what they assume will be unpalatable. Since they are likely to regard the Justice Department lawyers as being uninitiated in the ways of bureaucratic life, they are unlikely to state with any degree of candor the "real-life" administrative concerns and pressures that make the case important. The FAA, for example, has felt obliged to recommend appeals in tort claims cases charging its air traffic controllers with negligence resulting in plane crashes at airports. These cases turn on purely factual determinations unique to each case, and thus present little hope for appellate reversal. For the sake of organizational morale, however, FAA lawyers feel a responsibility to support the air traffic controllers by urging appeals despite the slim chance of success. In the early days of the volunteer army, Selective Service pressed for appeals in unimportant cases, apparently in order to keep its statutory authority in good legal repair should the draft ever return. The Internal Revenue Service has been known to argue for appeal where regulations have been found defective, solely because without an appellate court decision the IRS finds it excessively difficult to persuade others in the Treasury to modify the regulation. Still other appeals have been urged in order to placate or satisfy important interest groups which benefit from agency policies. Agency recommendations for appeal are not infrequently motivated by one or more of many such considerations never stated in the formal recommendations. Where this is the case, the agency's passionate defense of its action, supported by what appears to be logical hairsplitting, is likely to be perceived by Justice Department lawyers as irrational, indecipherable, or inexplicable. Unless they prove so far as to evoke a candid or unguarded response, they may very well miss the entire point of the appeal recommendation.

There is an additional problem of interpretation. Covert bureaucratic or political concerns can produce two entirely different kinds of appeal recommendations. As indicated earlier, the agency lawyers may urge appeal, fully anticipating that Justice will not agree, and there the matter will rest. Whoever inside or outside the agency pressed for a vigorous defense may not be satisfied, but at least he will know that the agency legal staff did "everything it could" for the cause. Responsibility for the decision not to pursue the matter rests in an organization beyond its control—which is exactly where the agency lawyers want it to be. But there are other cases where the agency lawyers do not advocate appeal merely to shift responsibility for not appealing; administrative problems impel them to urge appeal in order to obtain a more satisfactory judicial outcome. If these underlying pressures are left unstated, as they generally are, the Justice lawyer will often be unable to distinguish between these two quite different categories. The distinction may become especially important if some hidden administrative concerns have potential legal relevance and might ultimately be urged on a reviewing court in support of the agency's position. But this the agency lawyers may not recognize.

Second, just as the courts are perceived by the agency lawyers as being somewhat "unpredictable," so, too, are the Justice Department lawyers in deciding what and how to litigate. Being out of touch with judicial thinking, the agency lawyers are really quite unsure of what is likely to be a persuasive argument in favor of appeal. Their frequent tendency is to use many arguments, weighing every argument equally in the hope that one or more will be accorded a sympathetic reception and produce a favorable result—despite the fact that some arguments reflect concerns that are central to the agencies' business, whereas some reflect concerns that are at best peripheral.

This combination of filtering and makeweight arguments sometimes leaves the Justice Department lawyers with the sense that something is often being held back, but with very little ability to identify what it is. In the process of recommending whether to appeal, the Justice lawyer is likely, depending on what he *does* know about the case, to proceed in one of two ways. He may either go along in the dark, accepting the agency's stated reasons uncritically, or else proceed to recommend for or against appeal based on his own analysis without regard to any arguments the agency has advanced, or with only sufficient regard to discredit those arguments by putting holes in the makeweights. He is easily able to distinguish among arguments made by the agencies on the basis of their "legal merit." He is, however, quite unable to sort out agency arguments on the basis of administrative convenience, interrelations of programs or parts of programs, or any of the criteria that may in fact be moving the agency to press so vigorously for an appeal. As the agency lawyer is unsure of what will move the Justice Department lawyer to respond sympathetically to his case, so the Justice lawyer has little sense for what motivates the agency's concern for the case and what might actually happen to the agency's program should the adverse decision be allowed to stand.

The effect of this reciprocal lack of understanding has occasionally been to precipitate conflicts between agencies and Justice over the appeal decision, usually fought out in the Solicitor General's office and usually, as indicated, with Justice prevailing. The more general effect of incomplete knowledge of agency operations and the context in which the emerging law must function is also to push the Justice Department lawyers toward a closer identification with the courts and, concomitantly, to diminish their sympathy with the agencies whose interests they are bound to represent.

A similar tendency can be observed on the agency side. As the recommendations of the general counsels' offices are disregarded by the Department of Justice, as they sometimes are, they come increasingly to appreciate that there is not a complete identity of interests, sympathies, or even habits of thought between them and Justice. The consequence of one or more such experiences is to discourage them even further from sharing the burden of their genuinely felt concerns with the Justice lawyers who must, in the end, educate the judges in these concerns. In this way, behavior that initially stems from the divorce of functions serves to perpetuate and extend that same behavior.

Prosecuting and Defending Appeals

Nor is the situation materially different if the agency has won in the court below and an appeal is taken by the adverse party or if the agency has lost but an appeal is authorized by the Solicitor General. For reasons to be enumerated later, the government routinely defends appeals in cases that it has won in the district court or the court of appeals. There is in fact no formalized procedure for deciding whether to defend an appeal (or respond to a petition for certiorari) comparable to the procedure for deciding whether to appeal an adverse decision. The defense is simply undertaken as a matter of course. Likewise, once an appeal from an adverse decision is authorized, even over the objection of the Justice lawyers, it is prosecuted like any other piece of litigation. But the matter does not rest there. There remains the question of what arguments to make and what arguments to abandon on appeal. In some cases, this question may have been partly obviated by the Solicitor General's appeal decision, for he may authorize an appeal on some grounds and simultaneously decline to authorize an appeal on others. But this happens in only the smallest minority of cases, and even then does not resolve all the differences that may arise as the Justice lawyers study the case more closely in the course of preparing the appellate brief.[c]

Only then may they become aware of what seem to them to be the "holes" in their case, of the defenses that are tenable or stand a fair chance of being successful versus those that seem likely to be pierced. Only then will they have had a chance to "try on" the case from the imaginary seat of the judge and attempt to sense what his probable assessment of its merits, both legal and factual, will be. As the advocate's view of the case on appeal evolves, he may come to believe on close inspection that some arguments which were adequate in the district court cannot successfully be advanced on appeal, that some arguments not made or only weakly made in the court below will have to be relied on and elaborated, or that some new arguments being urged on him by the agency lawyers cannot be urged on the appellate court.

---

[c] It is an interesting commentary on the mix of advocacy and adjudication at Justice that, whereas an adverse decision will be scrutinized from all angles before an appeal is authorized, the appeal once authorized is pursued with virtually all the arguments that seem to make tactical sense.

It is the closer scrutiny given to the fewer cases that reach the appellate stage that creates the framework for an additional series of tensions between the agency lawyers and the Justice lawyers. As in the case of deciding whether to appeal an adverse decision, there is a marked difference of approach between the Justice and agency lawyers. It is the difference between the artillery and the front-lines mentality, the one choosing its targets, the other using everything it has. The Justice lawyer is by no means averse to using arguments he personally does not believe to be meritorious, but in general he will prefer to rely on a few well-chosen arguments rather than a greater number of less meritorious arguments. His fear is that the employment of makeweight arguments will taint the credibility of the whole case, whereas the agency lawyer, like many clients, may be more inclined to stand on his rights and defend what is his with all the weapons at his command. In this respect, his notions conform more closely than those of the Justice Department lawyer to the theory of the adversary process.

The agency lawyer may also prefer jurisdictional and procedural arguments to arguments on the merits of the agency action, which he is loath to have adjudicated. The Justice lawyer, however, may believe that the long day of procedural defenses, if not over, is waning, and he may prefer to rely on the merits of his case, lest the court sense that he is hiding something beneath the cloak of procedure.

However, there have been some notable exceptions to this pattern. Lawyers handling welfare litigation for HEW have been known to prefer arguing the merits rather than threshold issues, such as jurisdiction or standing to sue, and they have agreed to procedural arguments principally in order to accommodate Justice. The reason for this reversal of roles is that, by and large, HEW was not defending its own programs but rather state welfare programs said to contravene federal standards. Consequently, the agency's stake in the outcome of the litigation was tenuous—in some cases, it was not a party but only *amicus curiae* ("friend of the court")[d]—and some of the state programs being attacked were not necessarily regarded with great favor or sympathy at HEW. In addition, the agency lawyers' relations with the nonlegal staff were heavily colored by the staff's partisanship for welfare recipients, so that these were not cases in which there was great staff pressure to defend a program to the hilt.

I mention this example, despite its exceptional quality, to indicate the variations that are possible in Justice Department-agency relations, and to suggest that many of these derive from the configuration of bureaucratic

---

[d] It is not uncommon for the government, when it appears as *amicus*, to focus on the merits, rather than other issues, and even to do so in a relatively detached way. The courts are believed to expect a thoughtful, rather nonadversary presentation from the government as *amicus*, as an aid to their deliberation.

and political forces operating on the agency lawyers from inside and outside their departments. The general propensity is, as I have indicated, for the agency to rest rather heavily on procedural doctrine—perhaps partly because the agency lawyer knows or suspects some of the practical political accommodations that often form the basis for agency action, and he fears, with considerable justification, that if they are discovered by the courts, they may be found illegitimate.

The Justice lawyers may also perceive the need to narrow the scope of the agency authority being defended. If, for example, there is a constitutional challenge to the authority of the agency to act as it has done or proposes to do, the Justice lawyer, sensing the seriousness of the constitutional question, may seek to avoid it by a "limiting construction," that is, a narrow interpretation of the agency's authority so as to bring it clearly within the realm of constitutional validity.[26] Necessarily, the limiting construction narrows the penumbra of the agency's authority for the sake of preserving the core, and the agency may be unreceptive to such a "voluntary" abdication of its prerogatives.

These are some of the many issues on which decisions on litigating position are hammered out. In general, though not always, the agency's inclination is to urge a broad-based defense, whereas the Justice lawyer is disposed to prune arguments, both for tactical focus and for purposes of salvaging the half-loaf where the whole seems in serious jeopardy. On occasion, too, a suit may present the opportunity of winning a major legal point in a recurring area of litigation, provided the Justice lawyer is willing to disregard less significant arguments that might enhance the chances of winning the case at hand but not advance the government's overall position. Risks with individual cases for the chance of greater gains are taken every once in a while. The abandonment of arguments by the litigation lawyer may be seen by the general counsels as unwarranted "concessions" to the adverse party. And if, in the course of explaining his position, the Justice Department lawyer adds to the tactical considerations his belief that the abandoned argument is unsustainable as a matter of (court-derived) principle, the agency lawyer may be excused if he believes that his advocate is unnecessarily risking the agency's case for the sake of some murky principles not to be found in the law of his agency.

The tensions for the Justice lawyer, as well as between him and his agency clients, are heightened because of recurring doubts about whether the government is a litigant like any other. Is its purpose in court to win cases? And if it is not always that, what exactly *is* its role? There are a number of conflicting thrusts. The tendency of the rules of the game is to confer on the government the rights and duties of ordinary parties to lawsuits—but not quite. The government is given more time to answer complaints, take appeals, file briefs, and perform other rites of litigation.[27] At the same time, the Solicitor General's office has had a long tradition of moderating the pursuit of untrammeled government interest in litigation by declining to authorize certain appeals or espouse certain positions, even if they had some chance of success in court. This tradition has, to a limited extent, filtered downward within the Department of Justice. Beyond that, as I have indicated, the Department has not infrequently taken it upon itself to assert some arguments and not assert others, based on the principle of the greatest good for the greatest number of agency litigants. Contrary to the adversary ideology, this can result in the sacrifice of the interests of a particular agency in a particular case.

The dominant tendency is surely to regard the government as simply another party before the courts. The structure of the litigation itself, however, points in both directions. A lawsuit is necessarily a combat; and when one is attacked, the impulse is to fight back, marshalling all available weapons and resources. But the complaint always charges the government with some action that deviates from the public interest, and when courts decide against the government, they make a determination that such accusations have at least some merit. The litigation lawyer, placed between the courts and his client, can hardly avoid the role of interpreter of such decisions to the interested party he represents.[28] The Justice Department lawyer thus sees any given agency case as part of a flow and part of a dialectic between the government and the courts. Like most clients, the agency lawyer and, even more, his colleagues in the agency assume that the single role of the barrister is to win. Most of the time, this is also the Justice lawyer's view. But some doubt is cast on this role by the Department's own avowed standards, by its representation of a range of agencies and departments, and by its intermediate position between the courts and its clients.

Because of these shades of difference in approach and role, as well as the spillover of adversary relations in earlier cases where appeal recommendations have diverged, there is sometimes a certain friction in the relations between "solicitor" and "barrister" even when both have agreed on the defense of the appeal. This is not to say that mistrust and disagreement pervade the relationship of Justice to the agencies. There are many forces working toward commonality in their efforts, above all their common desire (most of the time) to win. When tensions arise, there are ways of smoothing them out. The agency lawyer may be convinced that some defenses, whatever their intrinsic merit, are no longer persuasive in court, or the Justice lawyer may be convinced of the "reasonableness," if not the "rightness," of the agency's position and therefore feel obliged to put it before the court. In other words, mutual accommodation based on expertise and the representative role operates as a balm and a lubricant of unified action. The point is not that there is so much tension that it threatens to get out of control—there is, in fact, relatively little. It is rather that what little tension there is casts Justice every so often in the role of "friendly enemy" of the agencies it defends.

Among other things, this fact, together with the fact that the Justice lawyers are not within the agency's chain of command and hence for some purposes are "outsiders," operates again to inhibit the full sharing of information if there is a possibility that the information might prejudice or embarrass the agency in any way. Moreover, since the information in question is necessarily "extralegal," it is by no means clear just what information might be useful in advancing the lawsuit, or in what way. It should be remembered that the agency lawyers often have very little guidance in anticipating judicial behavior. Nor do the courts or the Justice lawyers really know what to ask the agencies for, despite the fact that both of them may entertain an uneasy feeling that they would like to know more about the agency and program at issue. In short, those who might have a sense of its relevance, if they had the information, do not have it, while those who do have it do not have a sense of its relevance. [f]

Consequently, as the courts increasingly assume new burdens of administrative oversight, they do not simultaneously find themselves in possession of significantly more information about the agencies' milieus than they formerly had. Despite the high quality of their legal arguments, the Justice lawyers are rarely the aid to the courts that they might be. As a matter of fact, the lawyer for the adverse party often has an advantage over the Justice Department lawyer. If the lawyer for the party challenging the agency action practices regularly before the agency—as he often does—he probably knows the context of the program far better than does the generalist from Justice. Sometimes he can use this knowledge to his client's advantage, for he can attempt to show the court how the agency action presently before it forms part of a pattern of invidious agency practice,[e] or that the impact of a decision adverse to the agency can easily be handled by a few minor modifications in the agency's mode of managing its affairs. These suggestions may or may not be accurate. The point is that the Department of Justice lawyer, seeing each piece of litigation outside its total context, may have no way of knowing. Nor is it material that courts try not to act on unsubstantiated statements of general practice, if their accuracy is not conceded (and it will not be) by the Justice lawyer. The central fact is that, much of the time, the judge is left on his own to feel for the truth and hope that he has grasped correctly.

---

[e] I have heard negligence lawyers refer to a comparable practice of introducing formally irrelevant but damaging innuendo about the defendant's usual mode of operation as "putting the stink" in a case. They do not expect to win on innuendo alone, but they use the coloring it provides as context in which they hope the jury will view the case.

Notes

1. See, e.g., the oft-cited article by Maurice Finkelstein, *Judicial Self-Limitation*, 37 HARV. L. REV. 338-64 (Jan. 1924).

2. See especially the writings of Jerome Frank, *Law and the Modern Mind* (New York: Brentano's, 1930), and *Courts on Trial* (Princeton: Princeton University Press, 1949).

3. Lon L. Fuller, *Collective Bargaining and the Arbitrator*, 1963 WIS. L. REV., 3-46 at 17.

4. In a sample of challenges to agency action (see Chapter 2, note c), administrative agencies fared slightly better (in terms of the won-lost ratio) in the courts of appeals than in the district courts. But these were only *reported* cases. District court cases disposed of without opinion are virtually never reported, whereas the work product of the courts of appeals is almost always reported. For data on reporting of district court opinions, see Allan D. Vestal, *A Survey of Federal District Court Opinions: West Publishing Company Reports*, 20 Sw. L. J. 63-96 (1966). Thus, reported appellate cases include a substantial number of cases that were not reported at the district court level, and those, in turn, are likely to be heavily routine and therefore heavily supportive of the challenged agency action. Further, agency success rates are relatively high in the courts of appeals because government lawyers appeal so few cases. (Indeed, this selectivity derives in no small measure from apprehension of the stiffer standards often applied on appeal.) From this selectivity and systematic differences in reporting practices, I infer that the agencies' overall success rates in the district courts are considerably higher than in the courts of appeals.

The best appraisal of government success rates in civil litigation generally (nonagency as well as agency litigation) is that of Paul D. Carrington. Carrington found that only about 1000 of the 10,800 civil judgments rendered in government litigation in district courts in 1972 were adverse to the United States. In other words, the government prevailed in more than 90 percent of these cases. In the courts of appeals—this time using Tax Division cases only—Carrington's data indicate a government success rate generally between 75 and 80 percent. "United States Civil Appeals" (paper prepared for the Administrative Conference of the United States and the Federal Judicial Center, Feb. 28, 1973; mimeo.), pp. 2-3. My own data for challenges to agency action in which the agency was defended by the Civil Division suggest a somewhat lower success rate in the courts of appeals: 65 percent for 1971-72, excluding Vietnam war-related litigation.

5. Several years ago, the Civil Division created a small office of Special Litigation Counsel to handle this class of exceptional cases and presumably to give them exceptional treatment. See 1972 ATT'Y GEN. ANN. REP. 77-78.

6. Agency litigation in the district courts and, less frequently, in the courts of appeals is sometimes assigned to the United States attorneys offices, rather than being handled from Washington, when the questions at issue are principally factual or routine or when the Washington work load requires it. There is, however, a limit to the number of cases that can be farmed out in this way, particularly given the common lack of enthusiasm for civil cases on the part of many United States attorneys' offices. See Richard E. Cohen, "Justice Report: U.S. Attorneys Push Wide-ranging Study to Gain Larger Role in Law Enforcement Policy," *National Journal*, Vol 5, no. 48 (Dec. 1, 1973), p. 1786.

7. The statement is that of a lawyer at the Department of Health, Education, and Welfare, Feb. 12, 1973.

8. 42 U.S.C. § 1401.

9. For an example of altered tactics reflecting sensitivity to this, see Brief for the United States, p. 21 n. 10, United States v. Penn, 490 F.2d 700 (5th Cir. 1973), *rev'd en banc*, 497 F.2d 970 (1974), finessing a question of the retroactivity of the Equal Employment Opportunity Act of 1972, thereby abandoning a position that has been urged vigorously by the government on district courts.

10. For the fiscal year ended June 30, 1971, the average reversal rate for all circuits in civil cases to which the United States was a party was 21.3 percent; this is marginally higher than the reversal rates for private civil cases (20.7 percent) and for all cases (18.1 percent). *Annual Report of the Director of the Administrative Office of United States Courts, 1971*, p. 241.

11. For an example of an appellate court's flagellating the government for such inconsistencies, see Estate of Stauffer v. Commissioner, 403 F.2d 611, 619 (9th Cir. 1968).

12. Military Selective Service Act of 1967, as amended, § 10(b)(3), 50 U.S.C. App.§ 460(b)(3). See, e.g., Oestereich v. Local Bd. No. 11, 393 U.S. 233 (1968); Breen v. Selective Service Bd., 396 U.S. 460 (1970).

13. 28 U.S.C. § 2680.

14. 5 U.S.C. § 552 (1970).

15. As we shall see shortly, the government appeals about one case in four where an administrative agency is involved and about one in five of all its civil cases. Computed from William Edward Brigman, "The Office of the Solicitor General of the United States," Ph.D. thesis, University of North Carolina, 1966, pp. 60, 62. Private litigants tend to have slightly higher rates of appeal: for fiscal 1970, they were in the range of 27 percent. Jerry Goldman, "Measuring a Rate of Appeal," Research Report for the Federal Judicial Center (Washington, D.C., 1973; mimeo.), p. 8.

16. By statute, the Solicitor General may be assigned by the Attorney General to attend to the interests of the United States in any court. 28

U.S.C. § 517. He is, interestingly enough, the only figure in the Department of Justice who is required by law to be "learned in the law." 28 U.S.C. § 505. This phrase has its origin in the Judiciary Act of 1789, but then it applied to the Attorney General. The office of Solicitor General dates back only to 1870. By regulation, the Solicitor General is required to direct the conduct of government litigation in the Supreme Court, to authorize the taking of appeals and the filing of petitions for rehearing *en banc* and for extraordinary writs (such as mandamus), to direct the preparation of *amicus curiae* (friend of the court) briefs, and to survey and list the appellate cases in which the United States is participating. He is permitted to intervene in cases involving the constitutionality of an act of Congress. 28 C.F.R. §§ 0.20-0.21. It is these duties which give the Solicitor General effective power to establish the position the federal government will take in litigation and hence to decide between conflicting positions urged upon him.

17. For purposes of this and the following tables, the "Department of Justice" recommendation is the recommendation sent to the Solicitor General's office by the Civil Division, Appellate Section. Occasionally, the trial and appellate attorneys within the Department disagree on the recommendation. See Brigman, "The Office of the Solicitor General," p. 42. Once in a great while, such a disagreement explains the decision made by the Solicitor General. *Ibid.*, p. 43. But such cases are rare, and generally there is no disagreement within Justice, so it makes sense to focus on agency versus Justice Department recommendations as if the latter were always homogeneous. I should add that in certain other divisions of the Department (notably Tax) the practice is to encourage a certain amount of diversity by permitting attorneys even within the same appellate section to state their views on the case separately, in the judicial manner. Where that practice prevails, it is difficult to determine what *the* Department recommendation is.

18. Interview, Washington, D.C., Nov. 13, 1973. This lawyer added that, of course, he did not adhere to same presumption in recommending whether to pursue a case to the Supreme Court.

19. Brigman found that when an appellate section recommended against appeal or certiorari, its recommendation was followed in 98.7 percent of all losses in the district courts and 99.8 percent of all losses in the courts of appeals. Affirmative appeal recommendations by appellate sections were followed in 88.5 percent of all district court losses and 59.1 percent of all court of appeals losses. "The Office of the Solicitor General," p. 37. These figures, however, include recommendations from all the various appellate sections, such as Tax, Criminal, and Antitrust, as well as Civil, and therefore include many nonagency cases. See also *ibid.*, p. 60.

20. Paul D. Carrington found that the United States appealed about one-third of adverse district court judgments in *all civil litigation* in 1972. "United States Civil Appeals" (paper prepared for the Administrative Conference of the U.S. and the Federal Judicial Center, Feb. 28, 1973; mimeo.), p. 2. This figure includes all noncriminal matters, and therefore embraces cases from divisions other than the Civil Division (e.g., Tax, Antitrust, Civil Rights). This higher appeal rate squares with Brigman's finding that Civil Division cases are appealed less frequently than those of all other divisions. "The Office of the Solicitor General," p. 60.

21. Brigman, "The Office of the Solicitor General," pp. 35, 60.

22. *Ibid.*, p. 35.

23. *Ibid.*, pp. 62-64.

24. *Ibid.*, p. 75.

25. The Solicitor General is less likely, however, to take such an approach in Supreme Court litigation. Brigman, p. 75, notes, for example, that the Department of Health, Education, and Welfare was successful in obtaining authorization to seek certiorari in none of the twenty-four cases in which it recommended certiorari. *But see* National Association of Letter Carriers v. Blount, 305 F. Supp. 546 (D.D.C. 1969), *probable jurisdiction noted*, 397 U.S. 1062 (1970), *appeal dismissed*, 400 U.S. 801 (1970), in which the Solicitor General, persuaded (against what must have been his better judgment) to authorize a direct appeal to the Supreme Court, later thought better of it and convinced the Post Office Department to agree to withdraw the appeal. See also Carrington, "United States Civil Appeals," pp. 1-2.

26. For the doctrine of "limiting construction," see United States v. Rumely, 345 U.S. 41 (1953).

27. See Charles Alan Wright, *Federal Courts*, 2d ed. (St. Paul: West Publishing Co., 1970), pp. 68-72.

28. On the naturalness of a mediating role for lawyers, especially for lawyers with captive clients, see Harry Brill, "The Uses and Abuses of Legal Assistance," *The Public Interest*, No. 31 (Spring 1973), pp. 47-51.

5

Of Half-loaves and Whole Hogs: Counseling Agency Litigants

As the Justice lawyers litigate, so the general counsels' offices counsel. There is no formal provision by which the Department of Justice plays any role in the counseling process. On rare occasions, however—where, for example, there are important political overtones or where significant litigation is anticipated to arise out of action about to be undertaken—Justice may be called in on an ad hoc basis at the planning stage.[1] Even in such circumstances, it may be the Office of Legal Counsel, or some other Justice Department office not connected with the ensuing litigation, whose advice is sought. For the most part, then, the Department of Justice is counsel *for* the government agencies but not counsel *to* them.

On the whole, as indicated earlier, the general counsels' offices are pleased by the minimal amount of intrusion into their domain that this arrangement entails. At the same time, this arrangement means that those lawyers who are in close touch with the courts are unable to participate on a regular basis in the interpretation of judicial decisions affecting agency action to the agency affected. There is, therefore, less litigation-oriented counseling than there might be, and that which exists is not conducted by those whose primary responsibility is litigation.

Every so often, however, the Justice Department does become involved in counseling agencies to modify practices that have been challenged in court. These efforts at counseling are almost entirely ad hoc, therefore virtually random in their incidence, and often ineffectual.

Obstacles to Litigation-related Counseling

The frequent inefficacy of Justice's ad hoc counseling efforts during the course of litigation derives from a number of factors. One of the most important is the existence of fundamental differences of orientation between the litigation lawyers and the agency lawyers.

As I have indicated, the litigation lawyer, as an advocate interested in victory, must agonize over what arguments can be advanced in court. As an advocate for most government agencies, he must also assess the potential damage that may be inflicted by a single decision on the government's general litigating position. This, of course, inclines him to pursue fewer appeals than the affected agencies would like.

Actually, though, the role of the Department of Justice lawyer goes beyond these merely predictive considerations. Because he is in close touch with the courts and because he derives gratification from appearing at their bar, the Justice lawyer tends to internalize the norms for which the courts speak, and he is likely to regard with suspicion or hostility agency action that seems to contravene those norms or to confirm the judicial stereotype of bureaucratic intransigence or myopia. By dint of his professional training, reinforced by his routine experience, the Justice lawyer, especially at the appellate level, tends to identify with the federal judiciary and its output far more than with the problems of his agency clients. He is likely to hold in specially high esteem astute and progressive appellate judges, even those whose opinions are frequently adverse to the interests of government agencies. The litigation lawyer is prone to admire their bold role conception, their insight and "craftsmanship," their thrust toward legality in a maze of administration. Nor are these attributes merely to be admired in the abstract, but, if possible, to be emulated by the Justice lawyer. The courts are, in a word, his "reference group."[2]

This identification with the courts before whom the Justice lawyers appear reaches its apogee in the judicialized atmosphere of the Solicitor General's office. To some extent, this is a function of the responsibilities of that office to "adjudicate" appeal decisions and the special relationship the office has to the Supreme Court. But the judicial ethos of the office goes far beyond what might be required on a purely instrumental basis to carry out its manifest functions. It extends even to idiom, which is laden with the kinds of phrases found in judicial opinions. An unimportant case is described as having "no prospective significance," an unattractive case as constituting "a poor vehicle" for a court test; and a brief memorandum may begin, "I join in the unanimous recommendation for certiorari," rather in the manner of a concurring opinion in the Supreme Court itself.[3]

This degree of affect is, of course, exceptional; few Justice lawyers entertain the platonic role conceptions prevailing in the Solicitor General's office. But still the courts are the most important influence on the professional orientation of the Justice lawyers, and the courts operate formally outside the bureaucratic system in which the lawyers must operate.

What this means in practice is that the Justice lawyer out of court is by no means a devout partisan of "the government's position." Commitment to external reference models and professional standards tends to make professionals working in bureaucratic organizations more critical of the organization's practice and less inclined to conform to established organizational routines.[4] To this general finding, the Justice lawyer is no exception. Mindful of his representative responsibilities, he is still inclined to examine agency behavior for its propriety, that is, for its conformity to his idealized notion of legal norms as propounded by the courts.

Within limits, the Department itself tends to encourage an external or "cosmopolitan"[5] perspective. Its stated mission of screening cases, its position between the courts and the agencies, its recruitment—geared primarily to a noncareer corps—all tend to elicit from its personnel something approaching an outsider view of the Department's business. This is a characteristic of long standing. Writing in 1937, the then Attorney General observed:

> ... the Department of Justice, standing between the executive offices of the government and the courts, is given the added function of a "buffer" in the relations of the executive to the judiciary. The law officers, observed on the one hand by the judges and urged on the other by public officers or legislators, face obstacles of the greatest difficulty. In the circumstances they make poor partisans, a failing which has called upon them criticism since the earliest days.[6]

There are, within Justice, standing jokes about inequitable agency litigating positions, recurrent "horror stories" about the latest pieces of agency malevolence or incompetence, and undercurrents of dissatisfaction about having to defend the agencies against litigants with legitimate grievances.

Naturally enough, all this leads to a certain amount of "role conflict,"[7] which is neatly summarized in the remark of one Justice Department lawyer who was reflecting on the accomplishments of the Department. Taking the position that the Justice Department was one of the government's best "success stories," he cited as evidence

> ... all the old and bad doctrines we've been able to maintain for the government in the courts. And also we've been able to persuade a lot of agencies to modify their practices and kept them from appealing each time a court finds they've done something wrong. So on both sides we've done a good job.

If this statement suggests the existence of role conflict, it also hints at the manner of its resolution. Like many such conflicts, this one is managed by compartmentalization: in court, an unflinching advocate; in the office, a skeptical mediator between the norms of the courts and the demands of the agencies. And there, precisely, is the rub, for the agency lawyers are not generally bothered by such conflicts. They have others to concern them.

For one thing, as we have seen, they are typically older than the Justice lawyers, who are often recruited fresh from law school, where they have imbibed their professional norms, and who often stay at Justice only a few years; the agency lawyers are more likely career men, consequently more distant from their professional socialization and the accompanying fascination with the courts. Furthermore, the agency lawyers must respond to a variety of interests and pressures. They cannot afford to indulge their taste for the pristine purity of the law or the preferences of judges. They must first do the bidding of their clients, the program managers. For the most part, within the agency they are regarded as expediters rather than frustraters, but counseling a change in policy or practice often means saying a very emphatic "no" to someone in the agency.[8] They must, in addition, consult with Congress and anticipate the demands made on them by the congressional committees that oversee their affairs, and they must respond formally and regularly at the oversight hearings held on their programs. Often this means recommending the defense of a congressionally enacted program all the way to the Supreme Court if necessary, even if the Justice lawyers can find no argument that will "wash" in court, for the agencies well know that otherwise someone in Congress will be asking why the agency did not fight to the very end.[9] For some problems, in other words, there is no acceptable substitute for an adverse court decision. The general counsels' offices must also cope with the claims of organized interest groups, which often have powerful channels through which to make their influence felt. The "clientelism" which has frequently been observed in the federal bureaucracy is not absent in the general counsels' offices.

Despite its wide range of litigating responsibilities, the Justice Department is in the end answerable principally to only one exogenous institution: the federal judiciary. The degree of "political interference" in the Department's civil litigation is, on the whole, remarkably slight. If a program is modified in the course of litigation or if an administrative practice is abandoned, the administering agency, not Justice, will be held accountable, even if the initiative for the change emanates wholly from Justice. In short, the general counsels' offices, despite their much narrower, more focused responsibilities, are answerable to many organizations and personalities outside their own offices.[10]

If this were not enough to create tension in the counseling process, there is another circumstance to be reckoned with. The Justice lawyers *manage* essentially nothing. To protect their jurisdiction, they need only retain ultimate control over their own litigation. The agencies, by contrast, have the mission of managing the programs assigned to them. For them, litigation entails both manifest and latent consequences. On the surface, any legal challenge to their authority may affect their ability to accomplish their mission. Underneath, every such legal challenge also threatens their ability to manage and control their own program in their own way.

Part of what is at stake in every lawsuit, therefore—whatever the "merits" of the case—is the agency's desire to be vindicated, to prevail, to work its will on those who resist it. The agencies are generally more eager than Justice to fight, to appeal, and to petition for certiorari even in inconsequential cases and even to the extent of pushing lost causes to a judicial decision that may ultimately hurt their program. This tendency to fight to the finish is easily documented—in the Department of Agriculture's desire to appeal yet another decision easing the requirements for standing to sue, in Selective Service's determined defense of violations of its own regulations, in HUD's strenuous recommendation favoring certiorari to argue against judicial review of its decision apparently in violation of a statute, and so on. There is, in these and similar cases, an eagerness to show some recalcitrant tomato packer, militant draft registrant, or aggressive citizens' group that the agency is in command, that it, not they, will run its program.

More than just the desire to maximize authority flows from the managerial responsibilities of the agencies. Lacking these duties, the Justice lawyer is apt to be rather cavalier about the impact of adverse judicial decisions on the agency he represents. He is inclined to think that his agency clients "can live with anything" if only they will show greater adaptability. "Every decision creates problems," he is wont to say, and the agencies must simply work them out. This resignation to change, born of repeated and routinized litigation, is not matched by the attitudes of the agencies or their lawyers. What looks trivial to the Justice lawyer may look very important, indeed, to his agency counterparts. They see the interrelations of affected programs, as he does not, and they take their business seriously. If a court rules against them, they must make the required adaptations; they know the entrenched interests affected, and they do not regard imposed change as a matter of mere routine. It is not surprising that they should be less than complaisant when their advocate at Justice steps out of his accustomed role of representation to urge upon them a modification of programs or practices which, in their view, might still be avoided by a zealous presentation of their case to the courts.

While the agencies' responsibilities are more focused in that they deal with specific programs and areas of concern, whereas the Justice Department's crosscut programs and functions, there is, however, another sense in which Justice can be viewed as the narrower body. It is a law department, and a law department only. Litigation, however, touches relatively little of what many agencies do. It is true, of course, that the fraction of government business affected by court decisions has increased considerably in recent years, and will no doubt continue to increase. But, in the main, most agencies do not yet feel obliged to alter the contours of a program because a few lawsuits have been filed to challenge aspects of that program—unless those suits constitute a broadside against the whole program or a whole set of regulations. For many program managers, as one agency lawyer puts it, "the number of cases lost in court is analogous to goods lost through shoplifting—it is just a cost of doing business."

The division of labor between specialists and generalists also affects the legal perspective from which each side views a controversy in which both are involved. The Justice lawyer's ignorance of the bureaucratic and social environment in which judicial decisions operate is paralleled by the agency lawyer's ignorance of what the courts, beneath their legal parlance, consider important. "Lawyers," observes David Riesman, "learn not to take law seriously"[11]—by which he means that legal education, at least elite legal education, and certain kinds of law practice foster a cultivated, almost contrived, skepticism of legal rules. It is something akin to what Karl Llewellyn means by "situation-sense,"[12] a feel for the relation of the unique situation presented by any given case to the more general *type* of situation that a court will perceive it to represent. Much of the practical ability to predict judicial reactions derives from "situation-sense." In the nature of their roles, the litigation lawyer is apt to display more predictive sensitivity to judicial cognitive processes and normative orientations than is the agency lawyer. For this reason, the Justice lawyer is likely to temper his literalness in interpreting legal doctrine with an infusion of his estimate of what seems appealing or at least minimally acceptable to judges. He may incline to a certain skepticism about the extent to which judicial decisions are governed by legal rules at all. In a complex obscenity case, for example, it was the prediction of more than one experienced litigator that the Supreme Court would be looking for a way "to throw a bone to the anti-obscenity forces," and this case might be that bone. The Court, it was said, would "like the basic idea of the statute, and if they do, the details won't matter. They'll find a way to take care of the details and sustain the statute." In the event, these prophecies were apparently confirmed, for the statute was unanimously sustained over objections that it impinged unduly on the constitutional right of free speech.[13]

Though there are wide variations among agencies and individuals, the agency lawyer tends to be rather more literal about his statutes, regulations, and prior decisions than the Justice lawyer. In analyzing a legal problem that comes before him, he is likely to regard his statutory and regulatory provisions and the agency's interpretations of them as the fountainhead of its authority. Judicial decisions, despite their finality, are for him only a gloss on that authority. The Justice lawyer, however, is apt to reason in the opposite direction, from the general principles enunciated by the courts to the particular instances exemplified by the law of a given agency. Where the barristers and solicitors begin their reasoning not infrequently affects where they come out.

Finally, the specialist, by definition, has only a partial view of the development of legal doctrine by the courts. But it is quite commonly the case that challenges to administrative action are grounded in the more general principles and trends of judicial decision to which the agency lawyers pay, at best, passing attention. These rapidly evolving judicial developments may be in constitutional or administrative law, federal procedure, injunctions, or a variety of areas that crosscut the functional responsibilities of individual agencies.

More than that, the development of legal doctrine may be indicative of wider-ranging ebbs and flows of judicial thought that can be inferred only from contact with a fair sample of decisions across the board. An Agriculture Department lawyer specializing in the regulation of milk handlers or a Labor Department lawyer concerned mainly with the Labor-Management Reporting and Disclosure Act will unquestionably find it difficult to stay abreast of the evolving general law; in all probability, he will also lack "situation-sense" in cases that go beyond his province. Lawyers at the Post Office, administering a censorship system for obscene materials offered for sale by mail, could not be expected to be fully cognizant of the nuances and implications of free speech doctrines developed by the courts to regulate censorship procedures applicable to movies. What they found most relevant were analogies to the postal fraud statute which they also administered and which the postal obscenity procedures paralleled. Yet the courts cared little for these analogies. In the end, the movie censorship cases proved decisive.[14]

Perhaps the best illustration of this general point is the most extreme one, deriving from a combination of departmental specialization and insensitivity to general legal trends. Called upon in 1970 to rectify alleged racial and residential discrimination in the composition of draft boards, Selective Service proceeded to predict (and justify) its immunity from judicial intervention on the authority of *Martin v. Mott*,[15] a case arising out of the War of 1812 and decided in 1827! Needless to say, the Fifth Circuit Court of Appeals did not see the issues in these terms. It scheduled the cases for *en banc* consideration—a procedure reserved, especially in that uncommonly large and busy circuit, for the most exceptional cases. Then, fully 2½ years after they were originally submitted, the fifteen assembled judges managed to avoid the serious issues the cases raised by affirming one without reaching the merits and finding three others moot, all in a series of brief *per curium* orders.[16]

In point of fact, agency lawyers are generally more inclined than litigation lawyers to cite older cases and to rely on older legal doctrine. Partly this is because, in each of their bailiwicks, they have a better collective memory than the litigators; partly it is because they are a step further removed from changes in judicial thinking. These two factors operate in tandem to create a lag in the diffusion of judicial innovation.

Many of the considerations I have outlined converge when the agency lawyers and the Justice lawyers confer on pending litigation. Because of their divergent interests, experiences, reference groups, scopes of responsibility, clienteles, recruitment, and habits of analysis, there is often only a most incomplete meeting of the minds. The Justice Department lawyers, who are familiar not only with the particular lawsuit in the context of others but also with the prevailing trends and personalities in the specific court that will hear the case, are apt to inject tactical reasons for moderating the agency's position in certain circumstances. If, for example, an unappealing case on the merits seems to jeopardize the continued vitality of a procedural doctrine favorable to the government or to the agency in question, this prospect will surely be called to the attention of the agency lawyers, but they are unlikely to be moved by such "half-a-loaf" arguments which, in any event, do not aid them in preserving the substantive authority they seek to maintain in that case.

To put the point more broadly, the litigation lawyer typically senses the relation of threshold procedural doctrines to the (formally unrelated) merits of the case, and also attempts to salvage favorable doctrines of broad applicability at the expense of doctrines of more limited applicability. The agency lawyer is more prone to perceive little or no relation between threshold and merits issues and to give each separate consideration. And he cares little if a doctrine is broadly applicable outside his agency when what he is trying to preserve is the more limited doctrine conferring *his* agency's authority on it.

In short, the divorce of litigating and counseling limits severely the counseling and litigation-planning role of the Justice Department lawyers. Not only is this role confined to the interstices of lawsuits already begun and either lost or potentially lost, but the program managers in the agencies believe that they are already receiving quite ample and often very agreeable counseling. The task of the Justice lawyer is all the more difficult because he, like some other bureaucrats, has the burden of attempting to *stop* something from happening. But, because he gets involved only in the midst of litigation, for the most part what he seeks to prevent from happening has already happened, and momentum is against him.

Levers of Litigation: The Occasions for Counseling

There are, nevertheless, two junctures at which the Justice Department lawyers play a de facto counseling role. In both instances, their role is assumed in the context of pending litigation, and in both the role arises out of the possibility that the lawsuit may be lost. In neither is it anything more than a stopgap attempt to avert that possibility.

I have noted earlier that there is no formal mechanism within the Department of Justice for deciding whether to defend an appeal taken by an adverse party—in other words, where the government has been victorious in the court below. Under such circumstances, the defense of the appeal is routinely undertaken, in striking contrast to the elaborate procedure for deciding whether to appeal from a loss. In the latter situation, a completely fresh, thorough look is taken at the lawsuit, and recommendations are sought from the affected agency. Why the difference between these two types of decisions?

The reasons are only semiarticulated, but there seems to be a formalistic presumption that the government does not defend suits brought against it in the first instance unless its position has merit. When the soundness of the government's position is confirmed by a judicial decision, there is no occasion to challenge or review that presumption, but when the government does not prevail, there is every reason to consider carefully whether its position is well founded. As we have seen, this presumption is quite at odds with actual practice, for, except in the most unusual cases, the first-line defense is accorded the captive client virtually as a matter of right.

Even so, however, the fictitious presumption remains in force as long as the government wins in court, for it is also underpinned by a more realistic consideration of litigating strategy. If the Department of Justice were to scrutinize the cases it has won just as it scrutinizes the cases it has lost, it would no doubt find itself deciding not to defend a significant number of appeals. In fact, it would often be obliged formally to "confess error" in the proceedings in the court below—that is, admit that the decision in the government's favor was erroneous. Naturally, if it did this regularly, Justice would be acknowledging, to its own embarrassment, that inadequate scrutiny had been given to its cases in the first instance. It would also give frequent offense to those judges who had ruled in favor of the government, only to find the props pulled out from under their decision by the ungrateful victor on appeal. Accurately or not, Department of Justice lawyers sense from experience that many judges react most unfavorably to confessions of error in their decisions.

The same considerations occur to the Solicitor General, who, according to a former practitioner in that office, "is aware that to confess error will not only infuriate the attorneys who have handled the case for the Government below, but also the judges who have been persuaded to decide in the Government's favor."[17] Consequently, confessions of error are entered only very rarely in the appellate courts. Even if a loss is anticipated on appeal, it is generally thought better to let nature take its course by letting the appellate court reverse the decision in question rather than risk the enduring enmity of the lower-court judge who rendered it by freely admitting his error.

Despite these considerations, it remains possible in principle for any of the actors on the government side to challenge the wisdom of defending an appeal from a favorable decision. In the rarest cases, Justice Department lawyers have done so, with varying degrees of success. Such a course might result in a confession of error where there is virtually nothing that can be said in support of the favorable decision and much to be feared from an authoritative appellate opinion that might strike down an agency practice in the most sweeping terms. Nevertheless, the absence of a routinized formal procedure for deciding when to defend appeals from favorable decisions and the high costs—in terms of judicial goodwill—associated with confessions of error render such a course quite unattractive and unusual.

Still, the possibility of refusing to defend an appeal or the less costly possibility of persuading the agency that the case cannot be won on appeal without a change in the challenged agency practice gives rise to the first of the two instances in which the Justice lawyers may take an active part in counseling the agency. If the agency changes its practice while the appeal is pending, it may be possible to avoid the horns of the basic dilemma—that is, to avoid being impaled on either a confession of error or a loss on appeal—because the posture of the pending case may be altered by the agency's new action. That action could conceivably (1) render the appeal moot by removing the very basis of the complaint, or (2) prompt the appellate court simply to remand the case to the district court for further consideration in the light of the new agency action, or (3) be sufficient to satisfy at least the minimal demands of the adverse party so as to facilitate a settlement of the case before the appeal is consummated. All these possibilities, backed up by the ultimate sanctions of a confession of error by Justice or an adverse decision by the appellate court, provide the occasion for Justice to counsel the agency in cases which, although won by the agency in the court below, raise serious doubts that they can (or should) be won on appeal.

At this point, however, the fact that the agency has prevailed thus far in the litigation is apt to create substantial doubts within the agency about whether it needs to rectify a practice that has already passed a court test. Hence, unless the Justice arguments on the improbability of continued success in the litigation are especially cogent, most agency personnel are disinclined to consider Justice advice sympathetically under these circumstances. And so, of the two points at which Justice may move into an active counseling role, this is the less likely instance. It is certainly the less likely occasion for the Justice advice to be heeded and acted upon.

Far more credibility attaches to the Justice lawyers' estimate of the improbability of success on appeal if they walk into the agency's offices waving an already adverse decision. Having lost once, the agency can readily believe that it may lose again, though it may still be quite unwilling to concede that its position lacks merit. It is the predictive factor that carries the weight and constitutes the opening wedge for the counseling role of the Department of Justice—the more so since every loss will be subjected to fresh formal scrutiny about the desirability of an appeal. An agency that is adamant about adhering to its stated policy on one day can become subdued and compliant the next if a court decision intervenes.

Counseling in the wake of a disaster already encountered is therefore more probable than counseling in the face of a disaster merely apprehended. In this respect, a loss has three consequences that a win does not have. It precipitates a fresh examination of the case as a matter of organizational routine. It avoids the delicate problem of antagonizing friendly judges by confessing error on them. And it endows the Justice Department lawyers with somewhat greater credibility in counseling the agency to modify its practice.

Even in the face of a loss and the prospect of another loss on appeal, the agency and its lawyers may still not take the opportunity to change course. They may prefer to fight on to the bitter end, because they are convinced of their rectitude or incredulous of the prospect of losing again, or both. The pressures acting on agency personnel to favor a change of position derive entirely from the perceived consequences of the pending suit and the prospect that Justice may be less than sympathetic in future cases.

In the first place, if change is inevitable, most agencies would much prefer to change their own practices rather than having judges, who are unfamiliar with the agency and may be unsympathetic toward it or even outraged by its conduct, order them to do so. A change that is "voluntary" is an exercise of agency "discretion" rather than judicial fiat, and preserves the cherished autonomy of the agency. More than that, it stands less of a chance of encouraging other litigants to seek court orders against the agency.

Furthermore, the "voluntary" decision can safeguard agency interests that might be endangered by the spillover of unanticipated consequences of a rigid court order. Related to this is the potential breadth of the court order. Agency-initiated changes can be tailored narrowly to the bare contours of the subject of the litigation; court decrees may be broader.

Finally, from the agency standpoint, it is bad enough to have lost a case in a lower court; it is far worse to lose in an appellate court whose decisions are more authoritative and geographically more effective. It is therefore preferable to cut the agency's losses as early as possible if a loss in the appellate courts appears certain, for the agency may be risking a wide range of principles in any given lawsuit, principles that may be applied in future litigation against the agency. It is thus sensible not to risk important legal points in a dubious or especially unattractive case.

These are some of the arguments the Department of Justice lawyers may employ when it seems highly doubtful that a significant case can be won on appeal. By the same token, this is the principal occasion on which the Justice lawyers attempt to convey to the agency lawyers and their clients a fuller appreciation of the trend of events and thought in the judicial branch. Sometimes these arguments prevail, supported by the implicit threat of a no-appeal recommendation or possibly a confession of error. But they prevail much less frequently than one would expect from their bare tactical significance. Quite often, the agency will fight on, though defeat may be virtually certain, until the Solicitor General refuses to authorize the appeal or, more rarely, confesses error; or, if the Solicitor General has been moved, pressured, or ordered to prosecute or defend the appeal, as the case may be, the agency, represented by the Justice Department, may cheerfully march on to defeat. Why does it do so?

Better to Have Litigated and Lost than Never to Have Litigated at All

To begin with, there may be people or groups with an interest in risking defeat for the sake of some gain that cannot be achieved without defending the suit to the limit. If there are political constituencies with a strong interest in the program under attack, the defense may be pushed on even in the face of impending judicial disaster. This was the situation with a case involving the constitutionality of compulsory chapel at the three United States armed forces academies, where it might have been anticipated at a very early stage of the litigation that a defeat for the government was virtually inevitable. Nevertheless, with the lawyers for the three military services leading the line of march, the government pursued the case all the way to the Supreme Court, which denied certiorari, allowing the adverse court of appeals decision to stand.[18] In cases of this kind, it is politically more important to appear to have fought the good fight even in a hopeless cause than to abandon the practice without going to the barricades in behalf of the relevant constituency.

If, as I have said, the counseling influence of the Department of Justice increases after a defeat, there may be occasions when Justice lawyers find themselves secretly hoping for a loss so that pressure for change can be brought to bear on the client agency. That is not to say that they do anything less than their obligations as advocates require—only that duties and sympathies may diverge. The occasions are rare, but they tell us something about the friction points in agency-Justice relations.

The first such category lies at the intersection of law and personal morality. If the agency is perceived as imposing its own standards on a wider community under the cloak of a statute, many Justice Department lawyers are likely to have no enthusiasm for the cause. The compulsory chapel case is in this category, especially because the legal basis of the chapel requirement was, in the light of earlier Supreme Court decisions, so shallow.

Similarly, cases involving the dismissal of government employees for homosexuality or heterosexual relations outside of marriage on grounds of the employees' "unsuitability" for federal employment[19] typically evoke the same reaction, as do discharges of servicewomen from the armed forces on grounds of pregnancy.

In much the same category were the "Philippine widow" cases, raising the question of whether certain widows of Philippine servicemen were still entitled to receive veterans' pensions. The statute provided for termination of benefits upon proof of "open and notorious adulterous cohabitation . . . ."[20] The Veterans Administration had construed the termination provisions broadly and enforced them with a vigor out of all proportion to the importance of the issue. This suggested to lawyers at Justice that something more than fidelity to a congressional mandate was motivating the policy. Rebuffed in the courts, the VA continued to refuse benefits and relied on a statutory provision precluding judicial review of its determinations.[21] Use of the no-review provision to shield the VA from scrutiny of determinations that might be contrary to prior judicial decisions produced chagrin in Justice. Some Justice lawyers were reluctant even to advance the argument that judicial review had been foreclosed, and some earnestly hoped that the courts would administer to an officious and recusant agency a well-earned upbraiding.

Another class of cases in which an advocate may entertain the hope that the adversary process will vindicate his opponent relates to agency lethargy in adapting to new law. Agencies often persist in following rules of law that the courts have been in the process of changing. The general tendency in the departments and agencies is to read judicial decisions as narrowly as possible, both because of the conscious desire to minimize change and the unconscious insensitivity to change that distance from the judicial process breeds. As a result, the agencies tend to give more weight to judicial decisions that have been outdistanced by events than the courts themselves do. Thus, the armed forces general counsels' offices repeatedly turned a blind eye to the so-called *respondeat superior* cases, holding the government liable under the Tort Claims Act for accidents negligently caused by servicemen driving to and from new postings. Under traditional doctrine, the servicemen might not have been on government business, but the courts had long since held that they were. Never unstinting proponents of traditional doctrine, Justice lawyers were disinclined to appeal the later cases and far from unhappy when appeals that had been authorized proved unavailing.

The same problem arises when the courts overturn traditional doctrine as applied to one agency. The question then becomes whether the new legal rule will be applied to analogous cases arising under different statutes in different agencies. In *Goldberg v. Kelly*,[22] the Supreme Court held that an evidentiary hearing was required by the Constitution before welfare benefits could be terminated. Naturally, this decision had ramifications in benefit programs other than welfare—for example, in Social Security and unemployment compensation. Some agencies potentially affected by the holding sought to escape its impact by distinguishing their own particular program. Few seemed willing to apply the new rule without an explicit court decision relating to their particular programs, and Justice Department lawyers were not enamored of resorting to the judicial process to test the applicability of the *Goldberg* doctrine to each program on a piecemeal basis.

"Sympathetic facts" also detract from the litigation lawyer's untrammeled commitment to victory. An agency's insistence on its legal position to the point of ignoring the human problems involved in its litigation often leads Justice to view the agency as shortsighted as well as wrongheaded. The matter goes beyond mere personal distaste for harshness in the application of law. If an agency has been burdening Justice with an exceptional number of unimportant or unwinnable cases, a likely response when the burden begins to become unbearable is to pray for a loss in a watershed case that will finally dam the stream.

In the early 1960s, for example, the Social Security Administration had construed the disability benefit provisions of the Social Security Act narrowly, to say the least. The position taken by the Administration was later satirized by one lawyer as follows: "If the applicant for benefits can breathe, he can work; and if he can work, he is not disabled." Needless to say, the courts entertained a quite different view of the same statute. Courts all over the country were construing it so broadly as to distort the actual provisions of the statute. The judges were simply unwilling to permit government officials to save money for the Treasury at the expense of disabled persons. Nevertheless, the Social Security Administration doggedly adhered to its view of the act. Under the impression that Justice had not been presenting the arguments for the Administration's position strongly and sympathetically to the courts, its lawyers continued to recommend many appeals that were bound to prove fruitless. Here was a situation calling for a dramatic loss, and Social Security lawyers were invited to attend the argument of an appeal during which its position was to be stated as fully as possible. The result was predictable: the judges were outraged, the position was discredited, and the case was lost. Thereafter, though the exceptions were many, Social Security lawyers took a slightly more generous view of the statute and a slightly less aggressive view of their losses in the district courts.

Irrespective of whether they believe the agency involved to have exceeded its lawful mandate, Justice Department lawyers may simply find some cases personally distasteful. In the last years of the draft, the Selective Service System was regarded by some lawyers at Justice as being so inequitable in design and unfair in administration that cases arising under its various provisions began to raise questions of conscience for those assigned to litigate them. Some attorneys asked to opt out, but others did their best and hoped for the worst. The same kind of objection was felt, for example, in cases involving the hair length of military reservists (the unshorn were sometimes marked "absent" at meetings and ordered to active duty as a consequence).

In discussions with Justice, agency lawyers customarily justify their position by stating that it has been forced on them by their clients, the program managers, while Justice lawyers place the onus on the courts. On both sides, there is usually considerable justification for locating responsibility in these places, because both sets of lawyers tend to be relatively powerless vis-à-vis the program managers and the courts, respectively. Nevertheless, this four-actor system opens the way for a certain amount of "engineered reform." If an agency insists on taking a position it has been advised against by the litigators at Justice, it may be accorded the dubious honor of presenting its supporting arguments to the court and suffering the slings and arrows of an outraged bench. Delegating such litigating authority to agencies on an ad hoc, one-time basis in predictably unpopular cases is a time-honored and often successful way of sending a powerful message to the agency about the unsoundness of its litigating position.[23] When the agency lawyers are given responsibility for briefing and arguing the appeal, they can make no claim that an adverse decision was the result of inadequate presentation of the agency's litigating position. The "educative" value of such a loss is often used to inhibit an agency from burdening Justice with repeated requests for appeals to defend solidly entrenched but legally questionable agency practices.

In cases of this kind, Justice is seeking a ripple effect. The aim is to convince the agency lawyers that they disregard the Justice Department's advice at their peril, and so to make them more tractable clients in future controversies. As we have seen in the case of conferences in the Solicitor General's office, there are times when the agencies also try to achieve their own reciprocal measure of deterrence.

The groups willing to risk defeat may include some within the agency itself. Whereas Justice is a department run by lawyers, the influence of the general counsels' offices in the federal agencies is generally quite circumscribed. More often than not, the agency lawyer is a facilitator, a man expected to "find a way" to carry out the agency's mission, a yea-sayer rather than a nay-sayer. Not only may he have difficulty persuading his clients to abandon the defense of a suit brought against them, but he may actually have a personal stake in seeing that suit lost, so that he may use the adverse court decision as ammunition in his struggle for legality within the agency. The often weak position of agency lawyers may deter them from taking responsibility for significant changes in agency policy, even under the threat of litigation. But if the battle is fought to its inevitably adverse conclusion, not only will the agency lawyer be in a more effective position to use that court decision within the department in which he works, but his overall standing and influence may be enhanced once the program managers learn from unfortunate experience that their conduct may have highly detrimental legal consequences.

Thus, on some occasions, agency lawyers are pleased to have Justice wielding the no-appeal club against the agency; it relieves them of responsibility for saying what their clients do not wish to hear. On others, however, they may be obliged to contest Justice's advice while simultaneously hoping that Justice's jaundiced view of the case ultimately prevails in court. For example, there have occasionally been cases in which, contrary to the usual lineup, Justice argued that a procedural defense, such as lack of standing, might have a fair chance of keeping the courts from reaching the dubious merits of the challenged agency action, while the agency lawyers urged Justice not to rely on procedure but argue those very merits. In some cases, such a strategy might be invoked by the agency lawyers in order to end, once and for all, any uncertainty regarding the agency's authority. But where the agency is in all likelihood bound to lose on the merits, the more probable explanation for disregarding the Justice Department's advice is the desire for an adverse opinion which can then be used for policy purposes within the agency.

Like the Justice lawyers, then, the general counsels have an interest in using the threat and the reality of adverse judicial action to enhance their influence with *their* clients. But the more significant instances where agency lawyers have been unenthusiastic for the side of the case they found themselves on relate to the multiplicity of conflicting forces impinging on the work of the agency. Because of these forces, the agency may be under pressure to defend a lawsuit it would prefer not to defend. Department of Health, Education, and Welfare lawyers have not been entirely unhappy with court-ordered modifications in welfare law and practice, although these have had a considerable impact on its regulations. The HEW General Counsel's office has been cross-pressured. On one side have been White House and budget pressures against "liberalization" of the regulations; on the other, client and staff pressures in favor. Decisions either way could neither please nor alienate everyone. The Federal Highway Administration is more than a little interested in getting on with the job of building as many highways as possible, as fast as possible. When highway funds were impounded by the Nixon Administration, the Federal Highway Administration was every bit as unhappy as those who later brought suit against it to shake the funds loose.[24] Despite White House pressure on the agency to cooperate in defending the suit, there was a discernible amount of reluctance. Lack of enthusiasm to defend impoundment in court was common in the departments and agencies. HEW civil rights lawyers were perhaps equally sympathetic to those who sued them to compel more vigorous enforcement of the civil rights laws.[25] Many of these lawyers had joined HEW precisely in order to carry out that mission as diligently as possible. Undoubtedly, some in HEW had reservations about building a strong defense against the suit, and the defeat in court was viewed as a victory for the mission of the agency.

It is important to emphasize that the agencies' lack of sympathy for what are at least nominally their own causes derives from the structure of their external relations—with their clienteles, with others in the same or a different agency, with the administration in power. Similar lack of sympathy at Justice typically derives from internal considerations—repetitious and burdensome litigation, a litigating position regarded as hypertechnical, oppressive, or immoral, or a failure of the agency to keep abreast of new legal doctrine. Justice Department lawyers are simply not subject to the same external pressures that the agencies are, and, furthermore, they do not appreciate the extent to which the agencies bear burdens of this kind that Justice does not. This ignorance leaves them free to indulge their only recurring external influence—the courts. They are, accordingly, thoroughly intolerant of agencies that march to different drummers.

The fact that even their respective lack of enthusiasm emanates from different sources adds an additional element of friction to the relations between agency and Justice lawyers. It should be said, however, that the number of cases in which either side would not be disappointed by a loss is, as a fraction of the total number of cases, really quite small—certainly less than 10 percent—though they are often important cases. Despite the small numbers involved, as each side senses that there are classes of cases in which the identity of sympathies is far from complete, the relations *inter se* become to that extent more distant.

Knowing which kinds of cases the agencies do not care about winning means knowing something about which cases they will press only *pro forma*, which they will "cave in" on under only slight pressure from the Justice Department, which they may even not prepare with their customary diligence, and which court decisions they will accept and apply with more than the usual enthusiasm. Knowing which categories of cases the Justice lawyer dislikes means knowing which cases he will not want to appeal if they are lost and which he will try to use to turn the agency's policy around.

Singling out those situations that provoke a lack of enthusiasm on the part of government lawyers runs the risk of portraying the lawyers who nourish such thoughts as either so mindful of the public interest as to assume the role of ombudsmen or so faithless to their responsibilities as to ill deserve the designation of advocate. Neither portrayal would accurately represent the relationship of the lawyers to their cases. It is more accurate to view this phenomenon as a manifestation of the bureaucratic aspects of government law practice. These lawyers work in organizations that are in continuing relationships with other organizations. It should not be surprising that organizational considerations should sometimes pull them in one direction while the adversary process pulls them in another.

Counseling Outcomes: The Limits of Litigation

What, then, comes of this purely ad hoc, post facto counseling in the breach? Quite obviously, it is often resisted.[26] But it is sometimes tolerated, because the club of not appealing or of losing can have an impact on the interests of the agency. On occasion, it is actually welcomed as an attempt to rescue the agency from the embarrassing, potentially dangerous situation in which it finds itself.

The variousness of these responses suggests the wide spectrum of possible outcomes. There have been times when agencies, pressured and assisted by Justice, offered to compromise with the adverse party or rewrote large portions of their regulations under threat of litigation, thereby ending the challenge to their conduct by essentially conceding much of the merit behind the challenge. There have been other occasions, probably more numerous, where the agency deftly outmaneuvered the Justice Department lawyers by persuading, cajoling, or pressuring the Solicitor General or his superiors that a fight to the finish was in order.

In between these extremes, there are some strange accommodations possible. Perhaps the most bizarre involves the Civil Service Commission, which has authority to order federal agencies to remove certain federal employees for behavior that renders them "unsuitable" for federal employment. The Commission had consistently construed its authority to permit it to order removal of an employee for homosexual activity or for heterosexual activity outside of marriage. The courts had increasingly begun to make it clear that such behavior, provided it were off the job and not so notorious or deviant as to offend "community standards," was insufficient to warrant discharge.[27] Nevertheless, even though some of the affected agencies had little enthusiasm for dismissing competent employees on these grounds, the Commission persisted in ordering agencies to dismiss them, and the Commission's General Counsel persisted in recommending appeals when courts ordered dismissed employees in such cases reinstated. This was the practice until the force of the judicial decisions

became so strong that even the General Counsel had, finally but reluctant-
ly, to concede defeat.

It was thereafter understood that Justice would no longer defend such
suits, but it was apparently not understood that, for its part, the Commission would no longer conduct investigations into, or order dismissals for,
such conduct. The situation was thus transformed only so far as litigation
was concerned. Administrative practice on a matter admittedly turning on
a question of law already resolved was not altered to conform to the
norms accepted by the agency once the matter reached the courts. In such
cases, therefore, a federal employee's job came to rest, in an unusually
automatic way, on whether he had the interest, initiative, money, and legal knowledge to bring suit.[28]

This strange standoff provides an interesting illustration of the rather
limited impact that interstitial counseling by lawyers outside the agency
has on daily practice inside the agency. Judicial norms have generally
only seeped into the cracks rather than, as the courts might wish, flowed
into the main channels of administrative life. It should also be noted that
the limited effectiveness of the strong judicial decisions on the rights of
federal employees appears to derive in part from judicial ignorance of the
nuances of bureaucratic behavior in the Civil Service Commission—a de-
ficiency that the Department of Justice lawyers, hardly more knowledgeable on such questions than the courts, could not realistically attempt to
redress.

Of even more significance than the varieties of outcome in particular
cases are the more general effects of litigation-oriented counseling that
follows rather than precedes the litigation. Large corporations superficial-
ly appear to follow the government's practice of employing both "house
counsel" and retained outside counsel. But, on this point at least, the
similarity is more apparent than genuine, for retained counsel, while he
may assume the burden of such litigation as arises, also counsels regularly
to avert litigation.[29] Large private organizations, in general, counsel first
and litigate only as a last resort. For them, litigation is a kind of legal sur-
gery, to be dreaded rather than welcomed.

Although the federal agencies hardly welcome litigation against them,
to a considerable extent it would be accurate to say that the government
reverses the corporate procedure. While there is no hard evidence on this
point, the government's disposition to litigate challenges against it, rather
than resolve them by prelitigation accommodation, puts a premium on litigation and probably encourages adverse parties to seek solutions to their
problems with the government in court. For, like Justice, private parties
know that there may be at least a chance at modification of agency practice if the litigation begins to look dangerous to the agency. Since the

agencies are frequently insensitive to judicial thinking, many such suits are won, thus further encouraging resort to court. In short, the increasing flow of suits against government agencies and the increasing disposition of the courts to favor such suits may well be in part a function of the divorce of litigation from counseling.

From the agencies' standpoint, there are additional dysfunctions to this syndrome. Because of their distance from judicial developments, some agency lawyers counsel action leading to litigation, the results of which are virtually certain to redound to the further disadvantage of the agency. Thus, it was rumored that the so-called Hershey directive, which ordered local draft boards to declare anti-Vietnam war activists to be "delinquent" under the Selective Service regulations and hence liable to be inducted, was actually promulgated on advice of counsel. Suit was duly brought (by the National Student Association) and unduly defended, with the result that the court of appeals, in a celebrated decision, found the directive an abridgment of First Amendment rights.[30] This decision, and others like it, further undercut the legitimacy and fairness of the draft and the agency administering it at a crucial point in its history.

I have argued that such counseling as Justice undertakes is of only limited effectiveness, partly because of its ad hoc, quasi-legitimate character, partly because of the incomplete meeting of the minds that characterizes interactions between the litigation and agency lawyers. Yet the ability to counsel at all derives from the fact that the agencies are, by statute, captive clients, and it remains to be explained why the Justice Department's statutory authority is not a more powerful weapon than it is, especially in view of the desire at Justice to win in litigation and hence to screen out potentially losing or doctrinally dangerous cases. In this connection, I have already referred to the representative role of the advocate, reinforced by the fact that counseling is a deviation from the primary mission (and work load) of the Justice Department, namely, to litigate, and that the Justice lawyers' knowledge of both the structure of influence and the actual course of events inside any agency is really quite superficial. Two other factors are also at work.

First, the agencies are not entirely at the mercy of Justice. They may proceed to contest a threat made by Justice not to defend one of their suits, first to the Solicitor General and then (or perhaps simultaneously) to his political superiors in the Department of Justice or the White House, or both. Such applications are often viewed sympathetically. The agencies are, after all, members of the government "family" with "legitimate problems." (In this respect, they sometimes enjoy an advantage over outside litigants, even those with considerable political influence, who seek to affect the government's litigating position. The latter may be seen as "outsiders" who do not really appreciate the way in which government operates, and, of course, they have only a rudimentary understanding of standard operating procedures, so that they are unable to exploit internal bureaucratic forms to achieve their goals.) Beyond that, Justice has only "legal" arguments for its position, whereas the agencies may have administrative and political arguments that may—or may be anticipated to—carry more weight in the White House. In bureaucratic battles, Justice is apt to be perceived as excessively "legalistic." If, therefore, an agency is willing to push a matter to a political decision over the head of the Solicitor General, there is a good chance that it will prevail.

But not every agency is willing to jeopardize its relations with Justice by raising the ante in each case. On the contrary, the temptation to do so is certain to be mitigated by the knowledge that, come what may, the next case, too, will be handled by Justice. But the posssibility is there, and it deters officials at Justice from intruding very much into the affairs of its client agencies. The possibility is strongest, of course, in the most important cases for the agency, and hence it is often in these cases that the agency is least willing to be receptive to litigation-oriented counseling.

Second, the Department of Justice in general and the Solicitor General in particular must be careful to avoid creating the impression that they are not working on the "same team" as the rest of the federal bureaucracy. There is a limit to the frequency with which they can decline to espouse agency positions. This is a question of balancing the *duration* against the *extent* of power. Were the impression to gain ground that the Department of Justice or the Solicitor General were regularly "giving away" the government's position to those who challenge it, the Justice monopoly of litigation itself might be in jeopardy. Justice is exceedingly jealous of its monopoly, and there are agencies equally anxious to break it. It is neither uncommon nor irrational political behavior to avoid risking continued power by "voluntarily" declining to exercise it to its acknowledged limit.

Given the wide range of counseling outcomes, it is worthwhile to attempt to identify more systematically the variables that determine the success of a counseling effort by the Department of Justice.

Perhaps the most influential variable is the one mentioned earlier: the probability of losing in court. As the likelihood of a loss increases, the prospect of changing an agency practice also increases. But it increases disproportionately, indeed dramatically, as the probability of a loss begins to approach 100 percent. The relationship between the likelihood of loss and the likelihood of change is, in other words, not linear. I know of no policy change initiated by the Justice Department where the probability of loss was not assessed as being quite strong.

By definition, an anticipated loss has not yet occurred, and so much depends on the authoritativeness of a prediction of loss. A judicial pronouncement is, of course, more authoritative than the advice of a lawyer.

Thus, as I have said, a prediction of an unfavorable result on appeal, based on an already unfavorable result in the court below, is more credible than the same prediction not based on an already adverse decision. Likewise, if the agency has litigated the validity of a controversial practice and prevailed in the court of appeals, and the Supreme Court then grants certiorari, the agency will probably understand that its chances of sustaining the practice are slim.[31] This is indeed the stage at which a number of stoutly defended practices have been abandoned. For example, the Department of Defense practice of dismissing pregnant servicewomen from the service was finally nullified after it had been sustained by the court of appeals over the dissent of two judges who wished to consider the case *en banc* and certiorari had been granted.[32] The Solicitor General strongly advised the Defense Department to alter its practice, and only then was change forthcoming. Because of its expertise in the mysteries of that most mysterious of institutions, the Supreme Court, the Solicitor General's office commands the respect of agency lawyers second only to that commanded by the courts themselves. So the hierarchy of authoritative predictions runs from the courts to the Solicitor General to the lawyers in the Department of Justice, and also to some offices in Justice more than others.

But it is not merely a prediction that is made by the Department of Justice. There may be an express or implied threat as well. Justice may state its unwillingness to defend the contested practice in court. The agency's reaction may turn on how strong and how credible are the advice to change and the threat that underlies that advice. A number of practices that might have been changed had Justice been prepared to confront the agency with a threat not to defend it were not changed because Justice had qualms about using this weapon.

Justice, however, does not always speak with one voice: different offices within Justice may have differing reactions to the same issue. If the agency gets conflicting signals from within Justice, it may come to believe that its cherished practice is not yet beyond the pale and not necessarily in danger of going undefended in court. The Veterans Administration, for example, received exactly this kind of divided counsel from Justice on several such issues: attorneys in the trial office tended to be supportive of VA practices that appellate attorneys were attempting to modify. The VA successfully resisted. It is, therefore, not merely the strength and credibility of the Justice Department's messages, but also their uniformity, that may affect the agency's decision to stand fast or to change.

The level of court in which the litigation is pending also influences the prospects for change. Again, the relationship is curvilinear. In general, the agencies are somewhat more sensitive to the projected impact of a loss in the court of appeals than in the district court, but far more sensitive to the impact of a loss in the Supreme Court. (Similarly, the chance that the Justice lawyers will attempt to counsel a modification or abandonment of a contested practice is greater when the case is in the Supreme Court than when it is in the court of appeals, and greater in the court of appeals than in the district court.)

The frequency and timing of losses and anticipated losses are important factors affecting the likelihood of administrative change. A practice struck down by several courts in several contexts over a protracted period of time stands a greater chance of being altered administratively than one that has been struck down only once or twice (unless by the Supreme Court) or only in one circuit. But a practice invalidated more than once but in a short compass of time may still be adhered to tenaciously, whereas one held invalid in a well-spaced "line of cases" may be changed.

It is not merely that agency lawyers do not feel bound by one adverse decision or several in one court. (The Justice Department, incidentally, often also suspends final judgment pending more widespread judicial feedback.) Rather, it is a matter of reaction time. Just as the agency lawyers are prone to cite older cases than are the Justice lawyers, so are they slower to adapt to new doctrine.

For example, when the federal courts were in the process of liberalizing the requirements for "standing" to sue, the Agriculture Department found a number of its agricultural marketing orders under attack in the courts by plaintiffs who had not been granted standing by the Agricultural Marketing Agreement Act.[33] Predictably, the language of the act did not stand in the way of the courts, which granted standing to plaintiffs outside the ambit of the statute but clearly affected by the marketing orders.[34] Marketing orders are issued after administrative hearings are completed, and plainly it was in the Department of Agriculture's interest to allow participation at the administrative stage to those whom the courts were permitting to participate in the judicial review stage. This is a pristine case of a half-loaf argument: given Agriculture's inability to prevent challenges in court, there was a strong argument for permitting participation in an administrative hearing so as to forestall the claim in court that the administrative process was unfair—a claim likely to result in a *de novo* judicial hearing rather than review on an administrative record that Agriculture could shape to its liking. It proved impossible, however, to convince Agriculture that, though this was second-best to winning the cases outright, it was still "better" than allowing the courts to go all the way by first granting standing and then reviewing the marketing order *de novo*. There was more than one reason for Agriculture's hard-and-fast resistance, but one of them was that the Department of Agriculture lawyers had not had enough time to digest and adjust to the radically new, suddenly imposed, rules of standing. What is optimally required for change, in other words, is a clear "trend" of decisions. Whether a trend exists depends largely on the "density" of adverse judicial action, both in time and across courts.

Another variable also helps explain Agriculture's response to the marketing cases. If there is an important external constituency or clientele that has had an inordinate role in shaping the program or practice now in litigation, the prospects for change are dimmer than otherwise. Agricultural marketing orders are often heavily influenced by the commodity handlers whose incomes they affect. Allowing nonhandlers to participate in the process by which orders are promulgated could be regarded with considerable trepidation by the economic interests profiting from the existing procedures. Resistance could certainly be expected from this quarter. Where influences of this kind exist, there is an additional party who must be persuaded by strategic or half-loaf arguments for change.

The point should be broadened. Sometimes it is the influence of a congressional committee or of a powerful congressman or senator that inhibits an agency from "caving in," even when the agency would like to change course. Having the Department of Justice to blame for the change may be useful to the agency, but it is often not as useful as having a court decree to blame. Change is therefore less likely when any strong constituency outside the agency is able to make its influence felt.

The structure of relations *inside* the agency also matters. If the agency itself is divided on which way to go, there is, of course, no guarantee that these conflicts will be resolved intramurally. The top leadership of the department or agency may be preoccupied with other questions, it may be indifferent to this set of problems, or it may not wish to incur the costs entailed in supporting one side against another. In such cases, the courts may inadvertently become the battleground for problems that divide the agency. Advice from Justice, while it may provide ammunition for one side or another, may not be a powerful enough force to dislodge either of the contestants.[35]

The relative importance of the general counsel's office in the agency is another aspect of internal structure that may well affect the outcome. Often this is a matter of the personality of the general counsel himself, and whether he has been able to establish rapport with the top leadership of his department. In the cases involving the dismissal of federal employees for sexual misbehavior, discussed earlier, it appeared that the investigative arm of the Civil Service Commission had invested its influence in the continuation of the existing practice, and that the lawyers were relatively powerless to affect the outcome. Again, it is a matter of having an additional party who must acquiesce in the change. Obviously, change is easier to veto than to accomplish; the larger the number of diverse, interested parties (particularly parties whose perspectives are "nonlegal"), the less the likelihood that Justice's advice will prevail.

Then, too, there is the content of the policy to be adopted. Will it appear as a surrender to "immorality," to "godlessness," or to "special interests"? The sexual dismissal and compulsory chapel cases point to the importance of this possibility. The more explosive the issue is perceived to be, the greater the inclination to let someone else order the change. In such cases, it may also be harder to obtain an across-the-board recommendation for change—at least in writing—from responsible officials at the Justice Department; and, if one is obtained, it may still be difficult for the agency to assume responsibility for putting it into effect. After all, there may be newspapers, congressional committees, the White House, and segments of the voting public to answer to. Here, too, it is the intrusion of external forces, albeit in more diffuse form, that affects the outcome.

The magnitude of the proposed change and the publicity attendant upon its adoption are two further aspects of the content of the practice to be changed that may affect the outcome of a counseling effort. If the change requires fundamental modifications of agency procedure—for example, holding hearings where no hearings were previously required—the chances increase that someone in the agency will find countervailing considerations, perhaps unrelated to the particular practice at issue, that militate against change.

Similarly, if the change requires a public admission of an agency error, it is less likely to be adopted than if only a quiet turnabout is demanded. Hence a basic change in departmental regulations or administrative directives is less probable than a change that can be implemented without repealing or amending regulations or directives. Regulations are burdensome to promulgate and hence subject to the inhibitions of inertia and work load. The public process by which regulations are considered for adoption also draws attention to a policy that may have previously escaped the attention of some interest groups and politicians whose attentions may be unwelcome in the agency. For all these reasons, any change in writing is less likely than a change not in writing; a change applicable across the board is less likely than a change applicable to only one or two cases; a change that is, so to speak, de jure is less likely than one that is merely de facto; and a change that is affirmative—one that requires not only that the agency *stop* doing something but that it *start* doing something else—is less likely than a change that is purely negative. In short, at the extremes, a quiet abandonment of a quite specific old practice is far easier to achieve than the ceremonious adoption of a general new practice.[a]

---

[a] The proposed change in the agricultural marketing order procedure would have required formal hearings that otherwise might not have been required. This was a stumbling block. The outcome of sexual dismissal cases is equally relevant here, for it shows how much easier it was simply to stop referring such cases to Justice than to turn around the entire investigative procedure or to adopt new regulations.

It would be easy to infer from all this that the more important the issue, the more likely multiple external and internal forces are to be interested in the outcome, the more likely public, broad, and affirmative action will be required, and the more likely some obstacle to doing something will appear—and, therefore, the less likely an agency is to accept Justice's advice to change course on important issues. Plausible though it is, this inference is not necessarily warranted. The more important the issue in litigation is, the more likely it is to move up the judicial hierarchy and at some point to be carried to the Supreme Court. Rule 19 of the Supreme Court's rules of practice lays considerable emphasis on the importance of the issue as a criterion for determining whether a case is worthy of Supreme Court review by certiorari, and the Court's practice of reviewing cases of general importance has tended on the whole to conform to the guidelines of Rule 19.

What we are left with, then, are tradeoffs among at least nine variables:

1. the stated probability of a loss
2. the authoritativeness of the prediction of a probable loss
3. the strength, credibility, and uniformity of the Justice Department's advice to change and its threat not to defend
4. the level of court in which a loss is anticipated
5. the presence of a "clear trend" of adverse decisions
6. the existence of interested constituencies outside the agency
7. the relative importance of the general counsel's office and other interested parties inside the agency
8. the perceived "explosiveness" of the issue
9. the breadth, publicity, and affirmative or negative character of the proposed change

It is not immediately apparent from this list that "important" administrative practices stand either a greater or a lesser chance of being changed as a result of counseling from Justice in the course of litigation. What does seem to emerge is that there are many points at which change can be impeded. It is thus not surprising that there are many fewer instances of Justice counseling that succeeded in changing a practice than there are of counseling that failed to achieve that goal. Perhaps more significant, the existence of so many variables, and so many potential combinations of weightings among them, means that successes and failures in counseling are distributed in an almost scattershot pattern that bears little relation to either the importance of the issue or the merit of the underlying legal arguments for and against change.

Notes

1. See, e.g., the interesting White House perceptions of Justice Department lawyers compared to HUD lawyers in one such planning consultation reported by Martha Derthick, *New Towns In-Town* (Washington: The Urban Institute, 1972), p. 8. But compare what actually happened, *ibid.*, p. 16.

2. In the sense of being a source of his values and perspectives. See Ralph H. Turner, "Role-Taking, Role Standpoint, and Reference-Group Behavior," *American Journal of Sociology*, Vol. 61, no. 4 (Jan. 1956), pp. 316-28.

3. It is striking how much legal writing in general tends to resemble the style of judicial opinions. In part, this is instrumental; in writing briefs, for example, specialists in advocacy advise lawyers to write in such a way as to facilitate the lifting of whole passages into judicial opinions. See Karl N. Llewellyn, *The Common Law Tradition: Deciding Appeals* (Boston: Little, Brown & Co., 1960), p. 241. In part, it is a product of socialization, for law is generally learned through reading opinions. But it probably also reflects the extent to which, for some lawyers at least, the judge is the implicit reference model.

4. The literature on professionals in bureaucracies is large. See especially Peter Blau and W. Richard Scott, *Formal Organizations* (San Francisco: Chandler Publishing Co., 1962), pp. 60-74; Mark Abrahamson, *The Professional in the Organization* (Chicago: Rand McNally, 1967), pp. 60-62.

5. For the use of this term in organization theory, see *ibid.*

6. Homer Cummings and Carl McFarland, *Federal Justice* (New York: Macmillan Co., 1937), p. 510.

7. On the special susceptibility of "boundary positions" in an organization to role conflict, see Robert L. Kahn and others, *Organizational Stress: Studies in Role Conflict and Ambiguity* (New York: John Wiley & Sons, Inc., 1964), pp. 102-24, esp. p. 123.

8. See, e.g., Michael E. Abramowitz, "Bureaucrats and Lawyers: Legal Myths and Realities," *The Bureaucrat*, Vol. 2 (Fall 1973), pp. 256-68.

9. Thus, the same agency lawyer who professed great cautiousness about recommending that the Department of Justice pursue his agency's cases to the Supreme Court quickly added a qualification for cases involving the constitutionality of statutes. In these, appeals are vigorously urged on Justice, even where the probability of success is slight, largely because the agency would otherwise have to answer to a congressional committee. Interview, Washington, D.C., November 13, 1973.

10. Compare, for example, the divergent attitudes of the Justice Department and the ICC toward railroad monopolies. Samuel P. Huntington, *The Marasmus of the ICC*, 61 YALE L. J. 467-509, at 488-92 (1952).

11. "Toward an Anthropological Science of Law and the Legal Profession," *American Journal of Sociology,* Vol. 57 (September 1951), p. 128 (emphasis omitted).

12. Llewellyn, *The Common Law Tradition.*

13. Rowan v. Postmaster General, 397 U.S. 728 (1970).

14. Blount v. Rizzi, 400 U.S. 410 (1971). The key movie censorship case was Freedman v. Maryland, 380 U.S. 51 (1965). Compare the decision sustaining the constitutionality of the postal fraud provisions: Donaldson v. Read Magazine, 333 U.S. 178 (1948).

15. 12 Wheat. 19 (1827).

16. Sumrall v. Kidd, 468 F.2d 951 (5th Cir. 1972); Smith v. Leach, No. 27, 659, 5th Cir., Nov. 8, 1972; Cortes v. Local Bd., No. 28, 295, 5th Cir., Nov. 8, 1972; Lopez v. Local Bd., 468 F.2d 626 (5th Cir. 1972). A related case, argued and submitted *en banc* with the others, remained pending years later, the court having found a more satisfactory informal settlement of this troublesome issue than the device of the formal decree. Evers v. Williams, *appeal docketed*, No. 28, 181, 5th Cir.

17. Robert L. Stern, quoted by Arthur Selwyn Miller, "The Attorney General as the President's Lawyer," in Luther A. Huston et al., *Roles of the Attorney General of the United States* (Washington: American Enterprise Institute for Public Policy Research, 1968), p. 64.

Every so often a judge imparts reality to these fears. In one Selective Service case, the Solicitor General had indicated to the Supreme Court his reservations about the correctness of the court of appeals decision, and the Supreme Court duly reversed. The next government lawyer to argue a Selective Service case in that court of appeals received a lecture about the government's propensity to convince judges to adopt its position, only to abandon that position at the next appellate level.

18. Anderson v. Laird, 316 F. Supp. 1081 (D.D.C. 1970), *rev'd*, 466 F.2d 283 (D.C. Cir. 1972), *cert. denied*, 409 U.S. 1076 (1972). Admiral Moorer, then chairman-designate of the Joint Chiefs of Staff, had testified that "an atheist could not be as great a military leader as one who is not an atheist." *Washington Post*, April 29, 1970. Following the denial of certiorari, the three military academies abandoned the chapel requirement, with the admonition to the cadets at the Naval Academy "to take full advantage of your opportunities for worship and moral development." *Ibid.*, Jan. 6, 1973.

With far more legal ammunition, a similar fight in behalf of public funds for parochial schools was carried to the Supreme Court, amid considerable publicity about the President's personal commitment to the cause. See, for example, *Washington Post*, February 28, 1971. The cases are Lemon v. Kurtzman, 403 U.S. 602 (1971); Tilton v. Richardson, 403 U.S. 672 (1971).

19. See, e.g., Norton v. Macy, 417 F.2d 1161 (D.C. Cir. 1969); Carter v. United States, 407 F.2d 1238 (D.C. Cir. 1968). The "suitability" standard is contained in 5 C.F.R. § 731.201. *But see* note 28, below.

20. 22 Stat. 345, codified in 38 U.S.C. § 199 (1952 ed.), repealed by 71 Stat. 83, 163 (1957).

21. 38 U.S.C. § 211(a).

22. 397 U.S. 254 (1970).

23. See, e.g., First National Bank of Catawba County v. Camp, 448 F.2d 637 (4th Cir. 1971).

24. State Highway Comm'n of Missouri v. Volpe, 479 F.2d 1099 (8th Cir. 1973).

25. Adams v. Richardson, 480 F.2d 1159 (D.C. Cir. 1973).

26. Sometimes it even has a retrograde effect. There have, for example, been occasions when an agency's attention was called to the requirements of its own longstanding regulations, sometimes originally promulgated as part of an understanding with Congress, with the result that the agency was able to secure abolition of the regulations rather than comply with their requirements. Compare 32 C.F.R. §§ 1604.51-52, adopted in 1971, with their antecedents, imposing residence requirements for local draft board members. For the local board concept, of which the original regulations were a part, see National Advisory Commission on Selective Service, *In Pursuit of Equity: Who Serves When Not All Serve?* (1967), pp. 19-20. Some courts had begun to require strict compliance with the regulation. Compare United States v. Cabbage, 430 F.2d 1037 (6th Cir. 1970); United States v. De Marco, 2 Sel. Serv. L. Rep. 3204 (N.D. Cal. 1969); and United States v. Beltran, 306 F. Supp. 385 (N.D. Cal. 1969); with Czepil v. Hershey, 425 F.2d 251 (7th Cir. 1970), *cert. denied sub nom.* Czepil v. Tarr, 400 U.S. 849 (1970); United States v. Brooks, 415 F.2d 502 (6th Cir. 1969), *cert. denied*, 397 U.S. 969 (1970); Jessen v. United States, 242 F.2d 213 (10th Cir. 1950).

27. See the cases cited in note 19, above.

28. In 1973, regulations were proposed to alter the Civil Service Commission's policy of ordering dismissals for sexual misbehavior. See 38 Fed. Reg. 33315-16 (1973). In 1975, the Commission adopted new regulations and guidelines which tied dismissals for sexual misconduct more closely to the effect of the misconduct on "job fitness." See 5 C.F.R. §§ 731.201-202 and the guidelines in Attachment 2 to F.P.M. Ltr. 731. The new guidelines apply the same standards in judging homosexual and heterosexual conduct. The Commission made clear in its background statements that court decisions played an important role in these changes. See

U.S. Civil Service Commission Press Releases, Dec. 3, 1973, July 3, 1975. This suggests that court decisions and Justice Department advice may have an impact years after they are first rendered.

29. See Quinton Johnstone and Dan Hopson, Jr., *Lawyers and Their Work: An Analysis of the Legal Profession in the United States and England* (New York: Bobbs Merrill, 1967), pp. 303-06.

30. National Student Ass'n v. Hershey, 412 F.2d 1103 (D.C. Cir. 1969). The directive was contained in 32 C.F.R. Part 1642 (1968). I do not suggest that the rumor was true; it is enough that it was plausible.

31. Between 1948 and 1958, approximately two-thirds of all cases in which the Supreme Court granted certiorari were eventually reversed. Note, *The Court, the Bar, and Certiorari at October Term, 1958*, 108 U. Pa. L. Rev. 1160-1217, 1178 n. 184 (1958).

32. Struck v. Secretary of Defense, 460 F.2d 1372 (9th Cir. 1972), *vacated and remanded for consideration of mootness*, 409 U.S. 1071 (1972).

33. 7 U.S.C. § 608c (15).

34. Holm v. Hardin, 449 F.2d 1099 (D.C. Cir. 1971); Harry H. Price & Sons v. Hardin, 425 F.2d 1137 (5th Cir. 1970), *cert. denied*, 400 U.S. 1009 (1971). See also Rasmussen v. Hardin, 461 F.2d 595 (9th Cir. 1972), *cert. denied sub nom.* Kresse v. Butz, 409 U.S. 933 (1972).

35. Some court decisions have played such a role. It is said, for example, that the Supreme Court decision in Citizens to Preserve Overton Park v. Volpe, 401 U.S. 402 (1971), was a great victory for environmental forces within the Department of Transportation.

6

Pressures for Change: Emerging Challenges to the Division of Labor

In Chapter 2, I pointed out that among the props of the division of litigation and counseling are inertia and a sense on both sides that the present, imperfect arrangements are probably preferable to many of the possible alternatives. There are, however, other supports for the division of labor that do not depend on the preferences and apprehensions of the lawyers themselves. In spite of these, a number of challenges to the present arrangements have been emerging, particularly challenges to the Department of Justice's litigating monopoly. Here I shall identify some of the political underpinnings of the separation of litigation from counseling and describe some of the movements aimed at consolidating the two functions, at least in certain subject areas. These movements are currently more plentiful than they have been for some time, and there are signs that the time-honored division of labor is under stress, perhaps to an unprecedented degree.

Political Interests and the Division of Labor

Powerful forces favor the division of counseling and litigation, particularly the concentration of litigating authority in the Department of Justice. These forces have fought against infringements of the Justice Department's litigation monopoly. Justice itself is one such force. It has opposed bills in Congress that would delegate authority to litigate to particular departments and agencies. It has gone to court and to the White House to prevent agencies from usurping litigating authority. In *FTC v. Guignon,*[1] the Department of Justice successfully opposed an FTC attempt to obtain, on its own, an order enforcing one of its subpoenas. In *Leonard v. United States Postal Service,*[2] Justice challenged—unsuccessfully—the authority of the Postal Service to settle a case without its concurrence. The Postal Service had obtained statutory authority to settle, but not litigate, its own cases, and Justice went so far as to suggest that the Service might not even have authority to file a brief in support of its proposed settlement[3]—a suggestion that reveals how jealously it guards its monopoly of litigation.

In this Justice has some staunch allies. Among them is the White House, which has, from time to time, expressed anxiety about the danger of permitting agencies unsupervised access to court. When authority was given by Congress to the FTC to represent itself in any lawsuit, including an action to enforce a subpoena, the President threatened a veto, notwithstanding that the authority was contained as a rider to a bill high on the Nixon Administration's priority list, the Alaska Pipeline Bill.[4] In the event, the veto was not forthcoming, but the President delivered a broadside against such authority and implied he would work for its repeal.[5]

Continuing White House support for the Department of Justice goes much beyond the particulars of the FTC issue. As early as June 1970, at the request of Justice, the then Bureau of the Budget issued a circular to the heads of federal departments and agencies on the direction and control of litigation.[6] The circular was unequivocal in supporting the Justice Department view: "Legislative provisions on litigation, which departments and agencies incorporate in draft bills or recommend in proposed reports on pending legislation, should place litigating authority in the Attorney General, to be exercised as he deems appropriate."[7] The position of the Budget Bureau was that legislation should make action by the Attorney General discretionary, whether the agency was plaintiff or defendant. Departments and agencies were enjoined to oppose proposed legislation that impinged on "the Attorney General's litigative responsibilities or discretion."[8] In its examples of provisions to be opposed, the circular included provisions conferring litigating authority on United States attorneys rather than the Attorney General, as well as provisions conferring authority on agencies other than Justice. An administration firmly committed to centralized policy making and distrustful of the centrifugal forces influential in the federal bureaucracy extended this general orientation to litigation, as it did to many other matters.

To be sure, the White House has from time to time overruled the Justice Department in disputes over specific litigating *positions*, but it has been ardent in its support for Justice's general litigating *authority*. Like Franklin Roosevelt, who firmly planted this authority in the Department of Justice, later Presidents apparently believed that the Justice Department, if not necessarily more responsive to the general policy orientation of the Administration, was at least more amenable to central direction.

From the President's point of view, there are problems associated with this course. If the Justice Department lawyers have authority over litigation, they will, as we have seen, screen agency cases and decline to espouse positions that are far out of line with the pronouncements of the courts, whose intervention in such matters conservative administrations have generally deplored. But that is simply a cost of keeping litigating authority in one place, where it can more easily be controlled.

Putting the matter in these terms suggests the relativity of the White House position. Confronted with a choice of giving the Equal Employment Opportunity Commission (EEOC) power to issue cease-and-desist orders or power to bring suit, President Nixon chose the latter, regarded by business and the administration as the lesser evil. Under the 1972 amendments to the Equal Employment Opportunity Act,[9] the EEOC may bring a civil action to rectify discrimination in employment. Only when the defendant is a governmental body must the Commission refer the case to the Attorney General, who "may" then bring suit. Despite this exception, the White House has maintained a remarkably consistent position in support of Justice's litigation monopoly.

Justice has its allies in Congress, too. A provision confiding independent litigating authority to the proposed Food, Drug, and Consumer Product Agency drew considerable opposition in the Senate. An amendment was offered that would have transferred most of that authority back to the Department of Justice. Though it drew 31 votes, the amendment failed.[10] Ultimately, a Consumer Product Safety Act was passed, establishing a commission of the same name. Not only did the act leave food and drugs with the Food and Drug Administration; except in case of "imminent hazards," it allowed the commission to go to court only "with the concurrence of the Attorney General" or "through" him.[11] There remain many in Congress who strongly favor the centralized system of legal representation.

There are those in the courts who also favor a centralized system of representation. Federal judges see more Department of Justice lawyers (including assistant United States attorneys) than they do any other lawyers. Justice lawyers have an opportunity to develop rapport with the federal bench, which in turn relies heavily on them and their representations.[12] Justice has generally been given the benefit of the doubt where, as in *FTC v. Guignon*, the boundaries between its authority and that of an agency are vague. Indeed, Learned Hand went so far as to state that the presumption of Justice Department representation could only be rebutted by clear evidence of a contrary congressional intention.[13]

There are important reasons for this predisposition. Many federal judges recognize that the Department of Justice saves them work by screening out frivolous cases; in general, they are pleased by that practice. As Chief Justice Taft said in an early FTC case:

It was intended by Congress in providing this method of enforcing the orders of the Trade Commission to impose upon the Attorney General the duty of examining the scope and propriety of the orders, and of sifting out the mass of inquiries issued what in his judgment was pertinent and lawful before asking the Court to adjudge forfeitures for failure to give the great amount of information required or to issue a mandamus against those whom the orders affected and who refused to comply. The wide scope and variety of the questions, answers to which are asked to these orders, show the wisdom of requiring the chief law officer of the Government to exercise a sound discretion in designating the inquiries to enforce which he shall feel justified in invoking the action of the court. In a case like this, the exercise of this discretion will greatly relieve the court and save much unnecessary labor and discussion.[14]

The courts may respect the expertise of some agencies; they are less likely to respect their legal judgment.

Nevertheless, the judges are not unanimous in their preference for concentrated litigating authority. They, too, are aware that in some respects agencies can better represent themselves.[15] In a recent case, the Supreme Court gave a very narrow reading to the statutes conferring litigating authority on the Attorney General, quoting an early incumbent, William Wirt, to the effect that the Attorney General "does not sit as an arbitrator in disputes between the government departments and private individuals nor [sic] as a reviewing officer to hear appeals from the decisions of public officers . . . ."[16] But, plainly, that is exactly what the Attorney General and especially his delegates, the Solicitor General and his staff, do every day in the process of authorizing and declining to authorize appeals and petitions for certiorari, confessing error, and refusing to defend or advance certain arguments favored by agencies.

Too much should not be read into the Court's statements on this occasion, for the case involved an agency that wished to accede to the claims of a government contractor after exhaustion of the administrative process, but had been prevented from doing so by the General Accounting Office; the Department of Justice had then defended against the contractor's suit. The Court was transparently unhappy with Justice's role in thwarting action based on the agency's recognition that the contractor's claim had merit. Ordinarily, where the two disagree, the roles of the agency and Justice are reversed: it is Justice that finds itself acknowledging the rights of adverse parties against its recalcitrant agency clients. Were it confronted with these conditions, the Supreme Court would probably approve of a more expansive interpretation of the Justice Department's authority over its client agencies.[17]

Political motives vary. Administrations change. Public perceptions of agency missions and requirements shift, and these perceptions are likely to find their way into congressional sentiment. Even judges change their minds. Still, it seems probable that a wholesale attempt to eliminate or reduce drastically the Justice Department monopoly of litigation would meet with considerable resistance.

Some of the substantive congressional committees might welcome the opportunity to enhance their oversight of departmental business by enlarging the scope of departmental activity to include litigation. But a bill to reshuffle litigating authority across the board would have to go through the House and Senate Judiciary Committees, where the Department of Justice could, and doubtless would, make its will felt.[a]

Most important, such a proposal would probably be resisted stoutly by almost any national administration, regardless of party. It takes no special perspicacity on the part of a President to sense the propensity of agencies to gallop off in different directions and the concomitant difficulty of controlling them. The ability to locate responsibility in one place is a goal which has, and presumably will continue to have, great appeal in the White House. Centralized litigating authority is one of the few ready handles on the bureaucracy that a President possesses. Though it is, to be sure, a lever that is relatively rarely pulled, every so often control of litigation proves its value in a conspicuous way. President Nixon, for instance, was committed to federal aid to church-related schools. When the time came to support that position in court—a time that happily coincided with the 1970 congressional election—he had little difficulty inducing the Department of Justice to do so. Had he been forced to rely on HEW, there might have been much less enthusiasm for this position. The same responsiveness was manifested by the Justice Department in the defense of the impoundment of federal funds. Unlike many other departments, Justice has no interest groups breathing down its neck, able to thwart presidential orders. Its utility to a President thus derives as much from its dependability as from the convenience of having litigating authority in one place.[18]

Finally, calendar-conscious judges, not least the present Chief Justice, would be unlikely to acquiesce in a transfer of authority that left each agency free to bring suit and pursue appeals at will. The anticipated increase in cases filed and cases appealed would surely be large enough to generate audible objection from the bench.

Eroding Authority: Delegation, Usurpation, and Conflict

What cannot be done wholesale may nevertheless be done retail. There has been erosion of the Justice Department position over the last several years. Litigating authority has been delegated on a limited basis to several agencies. Some of these have been charged with responsibility for moving aggressively to bring some segment of the private sector into compliance with important goals articulated by Congress. As indicated above, the FTC and EEOC have been given broad authority to represent themselves.

---

[a] Interest groups would probably divide on the issue, depending on whether they regard the department or agency that handles their affairs as friendly or hostile.

The urgency of their missions outweighed the general proclivity toward concentrating litigation authority. There was fear in Congress of undue delay inherent in the need to refer cases to the Department of Justice and the possibility of "political manipulation or influence of Agency enforcement actions by administrative representatives . . . ."[19] Thus, the views of conservative Presidents have an exact counterpoint among liberal members of Congress: the latter may not like the policies of particular agencies, subject as those are to the inordinate influence of interest groups, but they also distrust the ability of the White House to control the Department of Justice. It is this distrust, coupled with bureaucratic and in some cases interest-group lobbying, that has permitted nibbling at the margins of Justice Department authority. In the apt words of the Somali proverb, "A force of cavalry will always find unguarded camels."

Not all the incursions into Justice's jurisdiction have been launched in order to give agencies with a social or economic change mission authority to bring suit. Some have been more mundane. A 1972 amendment to the Longshoremen's and Harbor Workers' Act explicitly allows Department of Labor lawyers to appear in proceedings under the act in any court except the Supreme Court.[20] This amendment, contained in an otherwise routine bill devoted to increasing the benefits and coverage provided by the act, repealed a long-standing provision for representation by United States attorneys. The language of the act creating the Postal Service does not grant litigating authority to the Service, but has raised questions about exactly what was intended. Under the act, the Justice Department "shall furnish . . . the Postal Service such legal representation as it may require, but with the prior consent of the Attorney General the Postal Service may employ attorneys by contract or otherwise to conduct litigation brought by or against the Postal Service or its officers or employees in matters affecting the Postal Service."[21] There are indications that the Postal Service may attempt to use the phrase "such legal representation as it may require" to obtain more than merely the sole authority to settle cases that was in dispute in the *Leonard* case, perhaps ultimately freeing itself altogether from the Department of Justice's supervision of its litigation.[22] A bill filed by a friendly member of Congress (and viewed with favor by the Postal Service) would have deleted the requirement of "prior consent" on the part of the Attorney General and permitted Postal Service lawyers to handle litigation on their own.[23] Plainly, the Service has been ardent on this issue. The Justice Department, for its part, is determined to resist: it has contended that the Postal Service statute does nothing whatever to impair the general litigating authority possessed by Justice.[24]

A number of other Justice-agency disputes have also simmered from time to time. The Small Business Administration, HUD, and HEW were not long ago reported as having tried to "gain control of litigation."[25] Attempts have been made to permit the Food and Drug Administration to conduct all its own litigation. Twice bills that would accomplish this have passed the Senate, only to die in the House, most recently in March 1976. Predictably, the Department of Justice has opposed this legislation.[26] But there is no serious resistance to the idea in the relevant congressional committees, and sooner or later the FDA seems likely to obtain the authority it has sought.

Other agencies may not have sought formal delegation of litigating authority, but that does not mean that they uniformly find the existing arrangements congenial. The various programs of the Environmental Protection Agency are serviced, for litigation purposes, by more than one component of the Justice Department. Those units served by the Civil Division were able from the beginning to work out an amicable relationship with Justice, partly because the first administrator of EPA had previously headed the Civil Division and many key lawyers at EPA had been recruited from that division, and partly because the Civil Division was satisfied to have some of its work load taken over on an ad hoc basis by agency lawyers whose competence it knew and respected. Those programs served by the Land and National Resources Division, however, have been in a different position. The Lands Division was not overburdened with litigation. To the consternation of EPA lawyers, it welcomed environmental litigation, with the result that relations between the Lands Division and the EPA have been characterized by recurrent tensions.

By far the most acrimonious such dispute was carried on over a period of years between the Departments of Justice and Labor over the Occupational Safety and Health Act of 1970. That statute provides, in splendidly ambiguous terms, that, except in Supreme Court cases, "the Solicitor of Labor may appear for and represent the Secretary in any civil litigation brought under this Chapter but all such litigation shall be subject to the direction and control of the Attorney General."[27] This language was modeled on the provisions of the Fair Labor Standards Act of 1938, which also allowed attorneys appointed by the Secretary to represent him in any litigation, with the proviso that the litigation would be "subject to the direction and control of the Attorney General."[28] As the Occupational Safety and Health Act (OSHA) established a statutory framework for the promulgation of standards designed to reduce the incidence of industrial illness and accident, so the Fair Labor Standards Act had done the same for the cause of minimum wages and maximum hours. It was only a matter of months before the Departments of Labor and Justice, through the good offices of Benjamin V. Cohen, were able to work out an agreement by which Labor would handle its own wage and hour cases but would give notice to Justice whenever a case involved a constitutional question or was carried to a state supreme court or a federal court of appeals.[29] In principle, Justice was to take control at the appellate stage. In practice, Labor represented itself, often briefing and arguing cases even in the United States Supreme Court. Private litigants quickly challenged this arrangement, but it was sustained by the courts.[30]

The ease and amicability of the Labor-Justice wage and hour agreement contrast vividly with the bitterness that attended the handling of the OSHA litigation. The wage and hour agreement was the product of the adventurous, cooperative spirit of the New Deal lawyers. The Justice Department monopoly of litigating authority was still relatively young, and there was no shortage of exciting legal work to go around. The lawyers at Justice and the agencies formed a fairly small, cohesive set of determined reformers with a common mission. Above all, if they disagreed, they retained their sense of being on the "same team" and did not lose sight of their conception that the private interests affected by the New Deal legislation constituted powerful adversaries to be fought by concerted action.

This kind of fervor is not altogether gone, but it is certainly much diminished. The jurocracy is far larger, more fragmented, and more diverse today than it was in the 1930s. The activist impulse and the single-minded consensus on the need to bring the private sector into conformity with national goals are no longer as widely or intensely felt in the federal legal establishment as they once were. Government agencies and departments recognize now, as they did not before, that challenges to their authority from within the federal government can be as dangerous to their survival and influence as challenges from without. Consequently, the litigating authority that was yielded graciously in 1939 was demanded gracelessly and retained stubbornly three decades later.[31]

As first drafted, OSHA did not make the Department of Labor's litigating authority "subject to the direction and control of the Attorney General."[32] Belatedly, Justice caught the omission in the legislative clearance stage and insisted on reserving the customary powers of the Attorney General. When, however, it was agreed that the OSHA litigation provision would be modeled on the Fair Labor Standards Act, Labor and at least some interested congressional staff had the impression that the same practice of delegating litigating authority to Labor would be followed under OSHA. In this they were badly mistaken, and the rudeness of their initial shock accounts for much of their subsequent vehemence in seeking to regain what they believe was stolen from them.

OSHA has generated a considerable amount of litigation, and the energy expended in gaining control of it for a while rivaled that spent in preparing the cases. Labor's first formal step was an appeal in 1971 to the Office of Management and Budget (OMB), based heavily on assertions that a bargain had been struck between Labor, Justice, and the congressional committees while the bill was pending. OMB found no evidence of such an agreement, and Justice evinced not the least willingness to accede, even as a matter of grace, to Labor's demand. L. Patrick Gray, later of FBI and Watergate renown, was then Assistant Attorney General in charge of the Civil Division. In the dispute before OMB, he was, by all accounts, "adamant" in defending Justice. Gray, who had spent many years in the navy, was accustomed to protecting his subordinates.

Justice argued that centralized control over litigation was necessary to achieve "consistency" among agencies that might otherwise pursue conflicting policies. It pointed to its litigation experience and its familiarity with individual judges. Finally, in Justice's view, there was a need to control the flow of cases reaching the courts and to establish priorities among cases. These were arguments that could hardly avoid appealing to the instincts of a central coordinating body like OMB.

Quite apart from these arguments, Gray's adamance was superfluous. In the face of the recently promulgated Circular A-99, OMB was not disposed to require Justice to do what OSHA, like the Fair Labor Standards Act before it, had made it a matter of grace to do or not, as the Justice Department saw fit. Nor did it hurt Justice that John N. Mitchell was then at the height of his influence as Attorney General. OMB was on the Presidents side, and the President was on the Attorney General's side.

For several years following the OMB decision, the Department of Labor attempted to undo the decision. Appeals were taken to the White House, to Congress, to the political leadership at Justice and finally to the Administrative Conference of the United States. Meanwhile, Justice handled the OSHA cases amid a campaign of vituperative protests from Labor, going not merely to the thrust of the Justice Department's treatment of the cases but to the minutiae. Labor was attempting to build a record of Justice Department noncooperation and inexpertness in the OSHA area, so as to render more plausible its claim on the litigation. Here was another case of an agency torn between its desire to win its cases and to have Justice lose them.

Finally, in early 1975, Labor and Justice negotiated what amounts to a peace treaty.[33] Two other statutes had been passed in 1974 permitting Labor Department lawyers to appear in court in cases arising under those programs, again "subject to the direction and control of the Attorney General."[34] Rather than extend the ongoing dispute over litigating authority to these new areas, the parties decided to end their hostilities. Justice agreed to delegate litigating authority in these three programs to Labor on a case-by-case basis subject to certain provisos. First, Labor acknowledged that "satisfactory cooperative relationships exist between the Civil Division of the Department of Justice and the Department of Labor with respect to the conduct of litigation under other statutes administered by the Department of Labor." In other words, Labor undertook not to challenge Justice's litigating authority in other areas. Second, Justice was empowered to retain litigating authority over all cases raising questions of constitutionality or of statutory interpretation and over Labor Department cases having a significant impact on other departments or agencies. Short of that, the expectation was that Labor would handle cases under OSHA and the other two programs in all courts except the Supreme Court.

The case-by-case delegation of authority that was to occur under this agreement fell short of the kind of blanket delegation that had occurred under the wage and hour program. Moreover, Justice did expect to retain some fraction of the OSHA cases, so the Labor Department's victory was not complete. The arm's-length character of the negotiations and the careful allocation of territory represented by the language of the agreement demonstrate how far apart the legal bureaucracies had drifted since the days of the New Deal.

The extended conflict served to confirm the beliefs each side entertained about the deficiencies of the other. An integral part of the Labor Department's tactics was to make multiple complaints about Justice's handling of its cases, the better to demonstrate the inadequacy of Justice Department representation. This led Justice Department lawyers to conclude that Labor Department lawyers cannot distinguish between trivial and important issues. Labor was also given, like many agencies, to overestimating the importance of every last case, thus leading it to recommend appeals in cases Justice regarded as insignificant. This reinforced the prevailing Justice Department belief that its screening of cases is an essential element in the government's litigation process. Labor also recommended and fought for adoption of some litigation tactics the Justice Department regarded as being of dubious utility, confirming in the eyes of the Justice lawyers Labor's lack of experience and judgment in dealing with the courts.

The Justice Department's handling of the OSHA litigation convinced Labor, on the other hand, that Justice had no political sensitivity (about the relationship between the Department of Labor and organized labor)—a fact exemplified by offhanded statements in Justice Department briefs; that Justice did not have the knowledge of factory conditions that is required to litigate industrial safety cases; that Justice was insufficiently deferential to the arguments clients wish to advance; and that Justice was too cautious and conservative in the way it approaches the courts, too unwilling to spend its credit for the sake of the case at hand. Clearly, issue was joined on questions of generalists versus specialists, court expertise versus program expertise, the interests of one client versus the interests of all.

Nevertheless, other agencies have swallowed what they, too, regard as a bitter pill. Why was the Labor Department so unusually persistent? Pointing to other interagency disputes Labor has had—for example, with EPA over whether Labor or EPA would promulgate standards to determine when workers might return to areas previously exposed to certain industrial dangers—some Justice lawyers have characterized Department of Labor lawyers as "empire-builders" busy "grabbing turf." The latter, using the same metaphor, have said that Justice Department officials were "protecting their turf" in pursuance of a kind of "bureaucratic *machismo*," a code that does not allow officials to yield territory voluntarily. There is some truth in these recriminations, but the reasons for the dispute go deeper.

As the lawyers at Labor saw it, the OSHA stakes were relatively high. They foresaw a large case load—ultimately, perhaps more than 200 cases annually. Like most agency lawyers, the OSHA lawyers do OSHA work and nothing but OSHA work: it is an all-or-nothing proposition. They are, moreover, in an office that traditionally has handled a certain amount of its own courtroom work, in the wage and hour area; and even where it has not, the office of the Solicitor of Labor has typically participated rather fully in the preparation of cases, often writing, in effect, draft briefs and, in certain cases, writing the briefs actually filed in the district court. Partly because of the frustrations of an active but only partial participation, partly because of its long-standing ability to recruit more able lawyers than many other agencies, the Department of Labor Solicitor's office has often been a difficult client for Justice, given to demanding litigating authority or at least veto power over the positions Justice takes in court.

There was something more, however. In some areas, the Department of Labor functions, so to speak, "adjacent" to the National Labor Relations Board, which does litigate its own cases. There is also some exchange of legal personnel between the two agencies. Several of the key legal officials in the Department of Labor had previously served in the NLRB, some of them in its Appeals Section, which handles litigation in the same manner as the Department of Justice does. OSHA is regarded, like the National Labor Relations Act, as an activist program, requiring vigorous, expert enforcement by a staff committed to OSHA and OSHA alone.[b] Indeed, like judicial review of NLRB orders, some proceedings under OSHA also begin, not in the federal district court, but in the court of appeals, some of them as petitions to review decisions of the Occupational Safety and Health Review Commission established by the act.[35] The autonomy of the independent regulatory commission exerts a strong pull on those who work anywhere near their magnetic field. For the OSHA

---

[b] The prominence of the NLRB as an implicit standard of comparison for OSHA lawyers is illustrated by their projection of OSHA case load figures by analogy to the growth of the NLRB's case load.

lawyers, the analogy to the NLRB was a compelling one that doubled their disappointment at having to funnel their cases through the Department of Justice.

There was, finally, the matter of recruitment. Those seeking litigating authority for the Labor Department believed they could attract and hold more able lawyers if they had the authority to go to court. This is a commonly voiced sentiment in government agencies, and we shall return to the question later when we also consider Department of Justice reasons for retaining litigating authority.

Agency-Justice Department disputes over litigating authority seem likely to continue. The fact that some agencies have recently acquired such authority makes others think it plausible that they might obtain the same authority. The conspicuous success of the Postal Service in challenging Justice in court and of the Labor Department in gaining concessions through negotiation both provide examples of what can be obtained. The low esteem into which the Department of Justice temporarily fell as a result of allegations connected with Watergate tarnished its reputation for impeccable professional performance. The increasingly heavy case load at the Justice Department makes it difficult to single out cases for special attention and probably multiplies the occasions for agency discontent with the way cases are handled. The continuing public criticism of agency performance and legislative attempts to reorganize the agencies or augment their powers provide opportunities to consider granting them litigating authority. The confluence of all these developments suggests that, for the first time in more than four decades, litigating authority may become an open question.

There have been very few attempts to move in the opposite direction, by giving the Justice Department counseling authority, but one such effort requires mention. In an inconspicuous regulation promulgated in July 1973, under the short-lived regime of Elliot Richardson, the Department of Justice stated that "No civil action against a federal agency under the Freedom of Information Act shall be defended by the Civil Division, the Tax Division or any other part of the Department of Justice unless the Department's Freedom of Information Committee has been consulted by the agency." The committee, in turn, was

instructed to make every possible effort to advance the objective of the fullest possible disclosure. To this end, in connection with its consultations with agencies that propose to issue final denials [of requests for information] under the Act, the Committee shall, in addition to advising the agency with respect to the legal issues, invite the attention of the agency to the range of public policies reflected in the Act, including the central policy of the fullest responsible disclosure.[36]

This regulation seemed to constitute a fundamental change in the division of labor. To be sure, the Freedom of Information Committee, in existence since 1969, had occasionally refused to defend Information Act suits against agencies, had also rendered gratuitous advice to agencies on their reponsibilities under the act, and had asked them to consult the Justice Department before denying requests for information. Its new role in counseling, backed by an explicit threat not to defend, was thus not entirely unprecedented. What was unprecedented was that this role was placed on a regular, rather than ad hoc, footing. An agency that did not clear a denial of information with the Justice Department in advance risked a refusal to defend. This was counseling with a vengeance. Against a background of agency recalcitrance in abiding by the Freedom of Information Act and judicial decisions interpreting it, the motivation for the regulation is understandable. But in its departure from the division of labor, this policy constituted a *coup de main*.

Besides being embodied in a regulation, the policy was enunciated unequivocally in a speech by Richardson and was reaffirmed strongly as a "commitment" of the Department by his interim successor, then Acting Attorney General Bork.[37] It was a policy difficult to repudiate for some time. Nonetheless, the regulation was finally repealed in March 1976.[38]

The adoption of a policy requiring consultation with the Justice Department as the price of being accorded a defense raises significant questions about the role of Justice in agency planning and decision making and the use of the litigating monopoly as a weapon to bring agencies to heel. True, the Freedom of Information Act cuts across agency lines, thus raising issues of uniformity of enforcement, but so do many other statutes. Does Justice have a counseling function, in advance of any litigation, wherever the matter concerns several or all agencies? Can it use its sole authority to litigate as a means to gain counseling supremacy? Put more dramatically, can it use the one half of the division of labor to obliterate the other? Many judges, one supposes, would be loath to grant such authority to the Department of Justice.[39]

The Freedom of Information Act regulation had been adopted without the approval of the line attorneys at the Department of Justice who had to administer it. They found it difficult to apply. There had been a significant increase in the number of suits under the act, and shorter time limits in which to respond. These made the required agency-Justice consultations so frequent and so hurried as to impair their value as screening devices. Ostensibly on these grounds, the regulation was repealed.

But more fundamental things were at work. With their limited knowledge of agency operations, Justice Department lawyers found themselves unable in a single conference to gain a full enough understanding of the context to help the agency decide whether to accede to a citizen's request for information. The regulation also forced the hand of the Justice Department lawyers, who preferred to make decisions in a case only after the "gradual unfolding of the facts" that occurs once litigation has begun.[40]

Finally, the Justice lawyers found themselves compromised by the consultation the regulation required. It appeared to put the Justice Department in a position of approving its clients' denials of requests for information under the act. This the litigation lawyers viewed as a modification of their detached position. They preferred to think of themselves as advocates, but not as partisans committed to their clients' decisions.

For this reason, Justice lawyers typically do not want general counseling authority. As a practical matter, Justice simply cannot get into the counseling business on a very large scale. The agencies are too many and too various, the Justice personnel too few. The threat of no defense in litigation, potent in some areas, is too weak in others. Furthermore, the cost in exposing the litigating monopoly to counterattack is potentially very high (see Chapter 7). In the past, agency lawyers could be confident that Justice had no real interest in the counseling process in advance of litigation. The agencies' counseling monopoly was the quid pro quo for Justice's litigating monopoly. But, with some agencies increasingly uncertain about the benefits of allowing the Justice Department to handle their litigation, an attempt by Justice to encroach on their counseling authority would accelerate agency demands for litigating authority. The status quo is fragile.

The precariousness of the present arrangements seems to impel Justice to emphasize the representative role at the expense of the screening role. This is not the time to take chances with client agencies. When a Justice lawyer was asked why the Department so often defended unsupportable refusals to disclose information under the Freedom of Information Act, he replied:

Everybody in government is constantly trying to get Congress to let his agency represent itself. Justice opposes that. . . . What's a poor Civil Division lawyer supposed to do? He's not an expert on [security] classification. Sure they [the National Security Council] were stonewalling. It's incredibly stupid. Sometimes we defend legal positions we wouldn't take for the [Justice] Department. But if you won't let your client defend himself, you've just got a lot of angry clients.[41]

These developments on the litigation and counseling fronts suggest that the division of labor may be in jeopardy for the first time since 1933. Ironically, most of the developments have relatively little to do with the increasingly interventionist proclivities of the federal judiciary that have called the present arrangements into question. They relate instead to congressional impatience with the Department of Justice, with the Department's own need to refurbish its image, and with the desires of agency lawyers to obtain the always-tempting power to represent themselves in court. But, whether causally related to new trends in judicial review or not, the current conflicts provide an opportunity to reassess the divorce of litigation from counseling.

Notes

1. 390 F.2d 323 (8th Cir. 1968). In this case, the FTC sought and was denied the Solicitor General's permission to petition for certiorari.

2. 360 F. Supp. 449 (D. Mass. 1973), *aff'd*, 489 F.2d 814 (1st Cir. 1974).

3. The statute conferring authority to settle cases is 39 U.S.C. §2008(c). The statute dealing with litigation is 39 U.S.C. §409(d).

4. 81 Stat. 576 (1973). See Judy Gardner, Richard Corrigan, and Joel Havermann, "Energy Report: Presidential Veto of Pipeline Bill Threatened Despite Fuel Shortage," *National Journal Reports*, Vol. 5 (Nov. 10, 1973), pp. 1693-97.

5. Press release, The White House, Nov. 16, 1973.

6. U.S. Bureau of the Budget, Circular No. A-99, "Direction and Control of Litigation" (June 30, 1970). The policy has been followed by the successor Office of Management and Budget.

7. *Ibid*., p. 1.

8. *Ibid*.

9. 42 U.S.C. §§ 2000e-4(b), 2000e-5(f). For the political background, see Karen E. Dewitt, "Labor Report: Strengthened EEOC Accelerates Action Against Business, Labor Employee Discrimination," *National Journal Reports*, Vol. 5 (June 23, 1973), pp. 913-21; Charles Culhane, "Labor Report: Battle over Enforcement Powers of EEOC Pits Business against Labor, Civil Rights Groups," *National Journal Reports*, Vol. 3 (Nov. 13, 1971), pp. 2249-59.

10. S. 3419, 92d Cong. 2d Sess (1972); 118 CONG. REC. 21879-89 (1972).

11. 15 U.S.C. §§2071(a), 2076(b)(7), (c). *Cf*. §§2060, 2061.

12. However, there have been complaints from the bench about United States attorneys. See Richard E. Cohen, "Justice Report: Senate Unit Drafts Proposal to Reduce Patronage in Staffing of U.S. Attorneys' Offices," *National Journal Reports*, Vol. 5 (April 21, 1973), p. 584.

13. Sutherland v. International Insurance Co., 43 F.2d 969 (2d Cir. 1930), *cert. denied*, 282 U.S. 890 (1930).

14. FTC v. Claire Furnance Co., 274 U.S. 160, 174 (1927).

15. See, e.g., FTC v. Guignon, 390 F.2d 323, 337-38 (8th Cir. 1968) (dissenting opinion).

16. S. & E. Contractors v. United States, 406 U.S. 1, 13 (1972), quoting Homer Cummings and Carl McFarland, *Federal Justice: Chapters in the History of Justice and the Federal Executive* (New York: Macmillan, 1937), p. 84. *But see* Cummings & McFarland, p. 490: "Where important questions of law or differences of opinion arise, they are customarily referred to the Department of Justice." Judge Shelton, dissenting in the Court of Claims, went so far as to suggest that the Department of Justice

had no more power than any other attorney representing a client. S & E Contractors v. United States, 433 F.2d 1373, 1387-91 (Ct. C1. 1970). This view is manifestly not in accordance with the Department's statutory authority or long-standing practice—for example, the power of the Solicitor General to decline to authorize an appeal requested by an agency or to authorize one not so requested.

17. Similar skepticism has been expressed regarding the Justice Department's authority to block a settlement favored by an agency, though not of the Department's authority to settle a case. Leonard v. United States Postal Service, 489 F.2d 814, 817 n. 7 (1st Cir. 1974).

18. The ultimate power of the President to control litigation involving the United States has long been established. See Albert Langeluttig, *The Department of Justice of the United States* (Baltimore: Johns Hopkins Press, 1927), pp. 112-13.

19. 118 CONG. REC. 21886 (1972) (remarks of Senator Magnuson).

20. 33 U.S.C. §921a.

21. 39 U.S.C. §409(d).

22. Interviews, Washington, D.C., November 27, 1973.

23. H.R. 11239, 93d Cong., 1st Sess. §2 (1973). This provision was buried in a host of minor amendments to the Postal Service law.

24. Brief for Appellants, Leonard v. United States Postal Service, 489 F.2d 814 (1st Cir. 1974).

25. Irving Jaffe, Acting Assistant Attorney General for the Civil Division, quoted in Richard E. Cohen, "Justice Report: U.S. Attorneys Push Wide-Ranging Study to Gain Larger Role in Law-Enforcement Policy," *National Journal Reports*, Vol. 5 (Dec. 1, 1973), p. 1794.

26. *Statement of Keith I. Clearwaters, Deputy Assistant Attorney General, Antitrust Division, Before the Consumer Subcommittee of the Commerce Committee Concerning S.2373, Proposed Amendments to the Food, Drug and Cosmetic Act, March 11, 1974* (Washington, D.C.: Department of Justice; processed), pp. 7-17. The more recent bill is S. 641, 94th Cong., 1st Sess. (1975). Inexplicably, the Justice Department expressed no public opposition to this bill.

27. 29 U.S.C. §663.

28. 29 U.S.C. §204(b).

29. Letter from Attorney General Frank Murphy to Elmer Andrews, Administrator, Wage and Hour Division, Department of Labor, Jan. 18, 1939, quoted in Fleming v. Cudahy Packing Co., 41 F. Supp. 910, 913 (S.D. Cal. 1941).

30. *Ibid.*; Lowell Sun Co. v. Fleming, 120 F.2d 213 (1st Cir. 1941), *aff'd*, 315 U.S. 784 (1941).

31. The 1939 agreement was actually extended to other areas at much later dates, but under special circumstances. Under the Equal Pay Act of

1963 and the Age Discrimination in Employment Act of 1967, the Justice Department agreed to delegate litigating authority to the Department of Labor. See the Department of Justice memorandum in 118 Cong. Rec. 21884. But the Equal Pay Act, 29 U.S.C. §206(d), was actually an amendment to the Fair Labor Standards Act, while the Age Discrimination Act expressly provided that enforcement should follow the mode of enforcement adopted under the Fair Labor Standards Act. 29 U.S.C. §626(b). So in neither case was there really a new concession on the part of Justice. OSHA, however, was a wholly new statutory area and therefore constituted a fresh object of conflict.

32. The description that follows is largely based on numerous interviews with current and former officials of the Departments of Labor and Justice and the Office of Management and Budget.

33. United States Department of Justice and Department of Labor, "Memorandum of Understanding," February 11, 1975 (mimeo.).

34. Employee Retirement Income Security Act of 1974, 29 U.S.C. §1132(j); Farm Labor Contractor Registration Act Amendments of 1974, 7 U.S.C. §2050a(d).

35. 29 U.S.C. §§655(f), 660(a),(b), 667(g).

36. 28 C.F.R. §50.9

37. *Address by Elliot L. Richardson before the House of Delegates, American Bar Association, Washington, D.C. Aug. 8, 1973* (Washington: Department of Justice, n.d.), p. 6; *Remarks by Robert H. Bork at the Interagency Symposium on Improved Administration of the Freedom of Information Act, Washington, D.C., Nov. 29, 1973* (Washington: Department of Justice; processed), pp. 2-3.

38. 41 Fed. Reg. 10222 (March 10, 1976).

39. See S & E. Contractors v. United States, 433 F.2d 1373, 1387-91 (Ct. Cl. 1970) (dissenting opinion), *rev'd*, 406 U.S. 1 (1972); Leonard v. United States Postal Service, 489 F.2d 814, 817 n. 7 (1st Cir. 1974) (dictum).

40. The quoted words were used by a Justice Department lawyer active in Information Act litigation.

41. Quinlan Shea, Jr., quoted in the *Washington Post*, July 26, 1976, p. A7.

7 Apportioning Authority to Litigate

Before considering the possibility of adjusting litigating authority, it is worthwhile to pause over some of the consequences of the present arrangements. The picture that emerges from our survey of Justice-agency relations has some rather disconcerting aspects to it. These relate both to the the process of judicial review of agency action and to the prospects for administrative legality.

For those given to unbounded confidence in the capacity of the judiciary to decide more and more issues formerly confided to administrators, there are grounds for at least a spasm of doubt. The Justice Department's frequent lack of knowledge of the relation of lawsuits to programs and the agencies' equal ignorance of the relevance of "program facts" to lawsuits are surely reflected in at least a proportional absence of informed judgment in the courts. As more and more government programs are created, and more and more questions about those programs find their way to the courts, lawyers at the Department of Justice become progressively less able to provide the specific materials needed for decision without themselves becoming the specialists that the agency lawyers are. The problem is exacerbated by the proclivity at Justice to emphasize recurrent rather than unusual issues in litigation and to present them in an accustomed fashion, according to its repertoire. Not only are the facts often incompletely or inappropriately presented, but the legal arguments, too, are sometimes filtered and skewed toward those of great generality. Generalists are not prone to emphasize what is unique about a controversy.

For those concerned with administrative fidelity to law, the questionable effectiveness of judicial efforts to bring the agencies to heel is repeatedly revealed by the mechanical and minimal way in which many agencies interpret judicially imposed requirements. The inability of Justice to turn experience derived from litigation into advice and, even more, into action in the agencies is manifest. As the agency lawyer has an imperfect grasp of what moves the courts to action, the Justice Department lawyer has an equally slight grip on the inner workings of his client agencies.

There is good reason to doubt the sanguine view of meliorist judges that, if the courts "have the will to create an effective system of law to guide and channel administrative decisionmaking," they can effectively eliminate administrative discretion.[1] So far, the tendency in the agencies to wait for a court to strike down an agency practice rather than to take the initiative internally suggests that court decisions are not having the ripple effect that is necessary if judge-made law is to guide action, for surely the courts cannot decide more than a small fraction of such cases. The inclination to leave such matters to the courts is, of course, greatly buttressed by the divorce of litigation from counseling, because it places the counselors two steps removed from the outcome, thus making responsibility that much easier to disclaim.

Indeed, there are even cases of noncompliance with court orders, let alone unwillingness to apply decisions beyond the cases in which they were rendered. Some years after enforcement of a National Park Service regulation had been enjoined, testimony indicated that the same regulation was still being used as the standard for Park Service decisions.[2] Similar instances can be cited in other areas, including, for example, disclosures ordered under the Freedom of Information Act.[3] This, too, bears on the division of labor, for a client's violation of a court order is the nightmare of the Department of Justice lawyer and no doubt of litigators in general. Yet, once the order becomes final, its effectuation is in other hands.

Judicial and Administrative Norms: Overlapping Responsibilities and Opposite Outcomes

If deviation from the thrust of judicial decisions still abounds, the courts should be absolved of guilt for showing insufficient quantities of that "will" which some judges hold to be indispensable to fostering administrative legality. The question is not so much one of will as one of structure. As we have seen with regard to counseling, it is not sheer obduracy that makes the bureaucracy less than fully compliant with the wishes of the federal judiciary. There are influential members of Congress, affected interest groups, determined political leaders, competing offices and factions, each with a distinctive conception of its mission. Under these conditions, the courts can hardly expect untrammeled deference to *their* conceptions of legality.

It is, in addition, worth asking whether we would like it if they had it. Do we really want to accord the courts a preemptive role in deciding whether agency programs are run in accordance with law, even to the exclusion of, for example, knowledgeable congressional committees? A compliant bureaucracy might in some respects be a less democratic one; it would surely be a less pluralistic one.

We are not yet at the point where we need to confront this problem squarely, and we shall not be there soon. The plurality of forces that shape administrative decisions does not appear to be in flight, and judicial power does not seem in danger of taking command of agency operations.

On the whole, given present levels of judicial activity, there is still too little, rather than too much, judicial influence on agency decisions. The courts and the government lawyers who appear at their bar are less proximate to agency decisions in the making, hence far less represented than other forces.

Of course, many questions can and should be raised about the proper role of the courts in reviewing administrative activity. But assuming the continuation of the generally interventionist proclivities of the courts, serious problems of fairness and consistency are created when judicial decisions affecting agency action are implemented only in litigation and not in the daily life of the agency litigants. As courts become more interventionist, the discontinuity between the law the judges apply and the law the agencies apply grows.

We have seen an example of this in the case of dismissals of federal employees for what the Civil Service Commission regarded as sexual misconduct. A discharged employee who brought suit was likely to be reinstated by the courts. After this trend of decisions had become manifest, the Department of Justice indicated its disinclination to defend such suits, and a discharged employee was often able to gain reinstatement by the agency virtually upon the filing of suit. But how many such employees lost their jobs and were not reinstated because they did not file suit?[4] This is an extreme example, but there are many less extreme examples throughout the federal bureaucracy. The common agency practice, referred to earlier, of capitulating in individual cases lost in court but going no further to comply with the rules enunciated by the court often creates manifest inequalities of this kind.[5]

There are other versions of grudging compliance, which produce slightly different varieties of inequality. An agency may decide to obey a court decree with respect to everyone in the relevant category within the locality in which the court sits—but nowhere else. An opinion in one circuit will not necessarily be implemented by the affected agency in another circuit which has not yet passed on the issue. Indeed, the agency and Justice may collaborate in setting up a conflict among the circuits in order to pave the way for Supreme Court review.[a] It has even been suggested that the Department of Justice has a "house rule" that a government position is not considered to have been rejected authoritatively until three courts of appeals have unanimously found it to be without merit.[6] Although I have never heard of any such tacit rule, it is surely no secret that Justice Department lawyers do not always feel bound to implement broadly one

---

[a] Rule 19 of the Supreme Court Rules lists among the circumstances that may cause the Court to look favorably on a petition for certiorari the fact that "a court of appeals has rendered a decision in conflict with the decision of another court of appeals on the same matter...."

or two, or even three, court of appeals decisions against them if they still believe their position to be defensible. Their clients are very much less disposed to feel bound by adverse decisions.

There are persuasive reasons for not always according court of appeals decisions final authority in government administrative behavior. The Constitution, after all, provides for "one Supreme Court,"[7] and the courts of appeals are not that one Supreme Court. To be sure, an argument can be made that a court of appeals decision ought conclusively to establish the law unless the government attempts to have it reviewed by the Supreme Court. But, in view of the many reasons for not seeking certiorari in every case—not all tactical—this seems to me an unduly narrow view.

Nevertheless, the fact that there are good reasons for not giving the courts of appeals the last word on matters of administrative practice does not mean that this custom has no unfortunate consequences. Quite the contrary. Recurrent reports of one result in court and another in the bureaucracy, on the same facts, can only heighten suspicions of administrative reluctance to abide by the law. These suspicions are often well founded.

There is some tension here between competing principles: the last word has not been heard until the Supreme Court speaks; yet the Constitution and the laws made pursuant to it are the "supreme law of the land,"[8] and inferior federal courts also have authority to decide what that "law" is. The Supreme Court cannot review every issue, even every important issue. Many issues must come to rest in the courts of appeals. The question that then arises is whether all issues must find their way to all eleven circuits before an agency concedes defeat and changes its policy. Even then, confronted with eleven adverse decisions spread across the circuits, some agency officials might feel bound to capitulate to the eleven specific litigants while still pursuing the same agency policy, so ill defined are the respective roles of administrators and judges in shaping the law and practice of an agency. More to the point, many officials are inclined to give themselves the benefit of virtually any doubt that may arise about the courts' reading of the law, even when the doubts are wholly conjured or fanciful. So inexpert are some agencies in interpreting judicial decisions and reading the judicial temper.

The problem does not end with the particular agency that has lost its case in court. Even if this agency applies the adverse decision vigorously and broadly to all those who are subject to agency action and similarly situated, whether or not they have been to court, there remains another issue of fairness and consistency. The sources of judge-made law tend to be of considerable generality. They emanate from precepts of and analogies to constitutional and common law doctrine, more than from the particulars of agency programs or activities. Beyond almost anything else, it is this dimension of legal reasoning that distinguishes judicial from administrative decisions and brings the courts into conflict with both the style and output of the agencies that litigate before them. If it is true that the sources of judges' law are general, it follows that their decisions are likely to have wide applicability—to other issues, to other programs, to other agencies. In many cases, it may not be difficult for an initiate to foresee how the standards applied to one agency's conduct would probably be applied by the courts to that of many other agencies administering a variety of programs. Are comparable agencies and programs equally bound by those standards, if no court has yet specifically held that they are? Are those affected by comparable programs equally entitled to be treated in accordance with those standards, court decisions or no?

These questions go much beyond whether the particular agency before the court must apply an adverse decision to anyone other than the individual victorious litigant, or whether it must apply adverse decisions in two or three courts on a nationwide basis. Yet there are compelling reasons for answering the questions in the affirmative. If the courts have the power to make and declare *law* in the course of deciding individual cases, as opposed to having only the power to decide those cases, then the rules they enunciate must have some counterpart in *behavior* that extends beyond the particular cases they decide. Consistency in the application of general principles is not simply an aesthetic value: it is part and parcel of what we mean by law.

The correspondence between the judge's law and the administrator's law will not be perfect. The cross pressures operating on the administrator are too numerous and varied for that. But the dangers of gross discontinuities cannot be ignored. Nor can it be assumed that the "worst abuses" inevitably find their way to court. There are too many extrinsic variables impinging on the decision to litigate to permit a confident assertion of this kind.[9] The search for consistency must go beyond court decisions, into agency behavior.

We know very well, of course, that different institutions judge differently. That is why we confide "administrative decisions" to bureaucrats, and not to judges; it is also why we require other kinds of decisions to be made only by judges and why some bureaucratic decisions are later submitted to judges for review. The very premise of the system is that decision makers who are recruited differently, who function differently, and who are placed in different sets of institutional relationships will provide distinctive contributions to the outcome.

But the putative virtue of this system of differentiated roles can easily turn to vice. It is one thing to say that different issues require different treatment and therefore must be handled by different decision makers. It is quite another to say that the same issue may find its way to different decision makers and be handled differently by them, resulting in divergent outcomes time and again.

Here is one of the largest problems of contemporary administrative legality. Paradoxically, it arises because of the increased efforts of the courts to call the bureaucrats to legal account. An active system of judicial review of administrative decisions enlarges the area of overlapping administrative-judicial responsibility—the issues which both will decide—and consequently enhances the opportunities for conflicting decisions and an arbitrary pattern of results.

The paradox is an extraordinary one. It goes something like this: The courts set about to redress the element of arbitrariness in administrative decisions by reviewing them more vigorously and meticulously. They arrive at different results from administrators, partly because they begin from different premises. The premises remaining different and responsibility for such decisions remaining divided, the two sets of decision makers continue to reach different results. The gap between the two sets of decisions on the same sets of facts widens, creating a generalized impression that similar cases end up with radically different outcomes. What begins as an effort to end arbitrariness merely substitutes one kind of arbitrariness—the unfairness of making the result turn solely on the forum in which the issue is decided—for the other kinds of arbitrariness under attack.

The principle that like cases will be treated alike reflects a deep commitment to a special species of orderliness—to an equality of outcome over and above an equality of process, even over and above the rightness of outcome. When the view gains currency that essentially the same case will come out differently depending on who decides it, and that this happens not occasionally at the margins of the decision system but recurrently at the heart of the system, the resulting attitudes must surely corrode the habits of deference to official judgment and confidence in governmental output on which democratic regimes depend.[10]

The corrosion is not far to seek. Speaking before a meeting of the Environmental Defense Fund, a former EPA administrator is reported to have told his audience "that he found it odd to be addressing a group that had sued him and the Environmental Protection Agency several times and won each case."[11] Lawyers would find nothing culpable about such an admission, particularly since EPA was a new agency, its authority and procedure largely uncharted. The official in such a position takes action (or fails to do so) and, if challenged, awaits confirmation or correction in court. But the columnist who was outraged by the administrator's statement, finding in it an illustration of "government lawlessness," was surely reflecting something besides his own naiveté. Why, he may ask, does judicial correction come so frequently? If the answer is that courts ignore the "plain meaning" of the law to further other goals, of what use are lawyers if they are unable to help administrators anticipate the nature and direction of those judicial departures? The point here is simple, but its implications are profound. The spread between what the courts are demanding and what the agencies are doing, even in good faith, can be wide. Those who regard courts as the sole oracles of law will find in this hiatus a pattern of government lawlessness. A consequence of this is to exacerbate public distrust of the bureaucracy and to erode the legitimacy of even those administrative decisions that do not find their way to court.

There is probably some circularity in this process. Judges themselves may very well imbibe the same cynical attitudes toward government agencies that are fostered by the earlier failure of those agencies to meet judicial demands, thus setting in motion a new spiral of demand and failure and heightened public distrust. I do not say that the ground under the bureaucracy is shaking yet, but it is not too soon to worry about the crevices that are visible.

That worry could go too far. It could create still another dilemma. If we ask agency lawyers to play an essentially anticipatory role, in a sense bringing the courts into the agencies through agency lawyers acting as surrogates for the judges, then we run the risk that the lawyers will "anticipate" things the courts would not require if the agency were permitted its day in court. So here, too, a balance is needed between too little court-oriented advice and too much, between an agency continually going its own way until a court tells it otherwise and an agency anticipating what the courts require and meeting those requirements without waiting for a lawsuit. Too much anticipation would make of the agency lawyers de facto judges—an office to which they have not been appointed. But, once again, present practice does not begin to approach this dilemma: there is far too little anticipation, not too much.

There is, it seems to me, a strong case for keeping the inevitable spread between judicial requirements and administrative behavior within limits. This argues not only for a court-oriented counseling system in the agencies, but for a program-oriented litigation process in the courts. Keeping the spread manageable ought to be a task attacked on both fronts. In this, the government lawyer is a crucial intermediary. Interpreter of the agencies to the courts, he is also interpreter of the courts to the agencies. The two roles are not easily harmonized, and at the moment they are performed by different functionaries. As we have seen, some of the difficulties of making the agencies responsive to the courts derive from differences of orientation between agency and Justice Department lawyers, and these in turn originate in the division of labor itself. Some of the problems the courts encounter in making sensible administrative law, both substantive and procedural, derive from the same source. What the courts most need is specialized information; what the agencies most need is a generalist perspective. Given the inevitable tension between these two goals, is it possible to restructure the division of legal labor so as to obtain more of both?

To Delegate or Concentrate?

Clearly, it is not possible to build broadly on the example of the Department of Justice attempt to counsel agencies under the Freedom of Information Act. The requirement that agencies clear in advance their refusals to furnish information with the Justice Department was possible only because this was a high-priority exception to routine practice. Even then, it gave rise to difficulties that caused Justice to revert to its earlier policy.

Establishing such a two-tier counseling process on a general basis would be prohibitively cumbersome, expensive, and productive of conflict. The Freedom of Information Act clearance procedure was based on a single key decision—denial of a request from a member of the public for information. In the totality of the government's legal work it is not possibly readily to identify a few similar pressure points. Some actions are negative, and some are positive. Some have an effect on individual members of the public, and some on the public at large. Some have an immediate effect, and some do not. Simply to clarify when an agency would be obliged to seek Justice Department clearance would itself be an enormous undertaking, certain to leave the gray areas far more numerous than the white or black. Its negative effect on morale in agency legal staffs would be formidable, and it would require a proliferation of Justice Department personnel.

On the benefit side, the gains of a centralized counseling system would be highly problematical. The Freedom of Information Act is patently a part of the "general law," not the "program law" which is the stock-in-trade of agency business. In dealing with the latter, even the agency lawyers and their clients do not always feel that the general counsels' offices are sufficiently enmeshed in the agencies' operations to understand the body of agency business their advice is supposed to affect. From time to time, proposals have been floated at HEW, for example, to place "solicitors" directly in operational offices rather than in a separate office of the general counsel. Justice Department lawyers, by contrast, are not in the agencies at all. From a distance, their ability to understand the program milieu in sufficient depth to counsel sensibly seems dubious at best. Even for litigation, which is more structured and focused than counseling usually is, the Justice generalists must continually be "educated" in the nuances of the relevant statutes and regulations. Their probable effectiveness in the more diffuse and politically complicated business of day-to-day counseling would not be worth the disruption it would entail.

Rather, a redivision of function must look tentatively in the opposite direction—toward the possibility of parceling out litigating authority to agencies. What are the arguments for and against such a delegation? In terms of redressing the deficiencies of the present system, what are the criteria that might be employed to decide if, when, where, and how to delegate litigating authority?

Typically, those agencies which have been eager for authority to litigate make several arguments. They assert what we already know—that the agencies have policy and program expertise that cannot be duplicated at the Department of Justice. They also contend that it is wasteful of legal resources, and often of precious enforcement time as well, to be required to educate the Justice lawyers, not only anew for each case, but for each step of the litigation (the complete separation of trial and appeal offices at Justice repeatedly baffles them). Where time matters, opponents of the agency know they can count on the delay inherent in this process.[b] Then, too, agency lawyers know the Department of Justice lawyers are often overburdened. From this they infer that Justice lawyers sometimes are unable to give proper attention to their clients' cases, sometimes make errors that less busy lawyers would not, and sometimes are forced to give lower priority to particular cases than those cases warrant. In some instances, the Justice Department perspective also leads to perverse assignments of priorities among cases, it is said, as well as to a certain amount of forcing of cases into a uniform mold. Finally, most agencies interested in gaining control of their own litigation are convinced that they could recruit better lawyers than they now do if only they could hold out the promise of going to court.

Justice, of course, argues that it is concerned to protect the interests of all agencies and, unlike some of its clients, will not sacrifice those interests for the sake of one case or one agency. The Justice Department is responsible for "the broad picture"; its mission is "to develop in court this unified approach."[12] Related to this is the general Justice Department belief that there is a virtue in uniformity and a vice in permitting agencies to espouse conflicting positions in court.[13] Justice lawyers are inclined to feel that valuable doctrines should not be put at risk for small gains, and that inconsistency from case to case, even if different agencies were to take the different positions, would bring less favorable results in court than a uniform position. On this view, Justice is not only the protector of

---

[b] This is a consideration of far more importance, obviously, in cases where the agency is plaintiff than in those where it is defendant.

the agencies' commonweal; it is also the monolith whose impregnability keeps hostile forces at bay.

A further reason for concentrated litigating authority is closely related to the first two. Justice argues that its function is to control the volume and quality of litigation by keeping weak cases out of court and, in the process, establishing overall priorities for what cases get to court. As we have seen, this role has been recognized explicitly by the courts. Justice sees the work product of the agencies on a regular basis. With some notable exceptions, Justice Department lawyers have little confidence in the ability of their agency counterparts to discriminate between what is persuasive and what is not.

There is also the argument from expertise. The pride of Justice is its understanding of the courtroom, the judicial temperament, the personalities of individual judges, and the customs and practices of the various federal courts. In the Justice Department view, the dispersal of expertise is a contradiction in terms; expertise comes from concentrated experience. It follows from this that, if the agencies could go to court on their own, there would be a net decline in the attention paid by courts to government lawyers and a rapid expenditure of the credit built up over the years with federal judges. As evidence, Justice Department officials cite cases in which agency lawyers have embarrassed the government or been ready to risk the wrath of certain judges by, for example, proposing a confession of error—a practice used by Justice only as a last resort.

And, of course, with respect to recruitment, just as the agencies hope to attract more qualified lawyers, Justice points to the fact that it already has them.

The Justice arguments are not new. The claim to expertise and detachment has long been the pride of the Department: "... attorneys of the Department of Justice, because of their very detachment from the business of administration, are equipped to interpret the laws and gauge the temper of the courts."[14] The argument for uniformity was the *raison d'être* for having a Department of Justice: it was to "secure uniformity of decision, of superintendence, and of official responsibility."[15] The current debate is, in short, a continuation of the nineteenth-century controversy over whether to centralize authority under the Attorney General. But while many of the arguments may be the same, the issues have changed. What is fundamentally different is the proliferation of agencies and programs as well as the qualitatively more important role of the courts in administration.

There are many points on which agency and Justice views are diametrically opposed. On recruitment, as indicated, Justice believes that a good lawyer in the hand is worth several still in law school, and in any case it doubts whether the agencies can attract the talent they think they can.

Justice would also defend the modification of agency priorities of which the agencies complain. As the body with the "whole view," functioning one step removed from the impassioned view of the litigation that prevails in the agency, the Department of Justice sees itself as the logical aggregator of multiple agency interests.

Nevertheless, on other matters the positions are not quite so antithetical. Agency lawyers may well concede the necessity to separate purely "parochial" questions—those that affect only a single agency—from more general ones, but they are quick to add that whether to refer a case of general importance to Justice should be the client's decision to make.[16] Justice Department officials might likewise agree that the most routine and perhaps also the most specialized cases could be handled by the agencies in which they arise (the same might be said for delegation of litigation to a few specially competent agency legal staffs). But the fear that pervades the thinking of Justice officials is that the consequences of the precedent for delegation would be inescapable: there are recurrent images of floodgates opening, feet in doors, and inches expanding into miles. These apprehensions lead Justice to favor limited delegations of authority solely at its discretion, "subject to the direction and control of the Attorney General."

As we move from the arguments for and against delegating litigation authority to the evaluation of competing policies, a caveat is in order. Not all agency general counsels would welcome authority to conduct their own litigation. Some are actively seeking it, some would accept it if offered, and some would rather leave it at the Justice Department. As we shall see shortly, these varying attitudes may have roots in agency circumstances relevant to the question of delegation.

Some extreme claims on both sides can be put to rest rather quickly. Consider first the matter of recruitment, often urged by agencies as a reason for seeking litigating authority. Although studies are conspicuously lacking, it seems that (remuneration aside) the ability of government departments and agencies to recruit talented lawyers is a function of three variables: (1) the intrinsic interest or social importance of the agency's mission; (2) the extent to which the agency's legal work has a counterpart in the private bar, so that government experience can be converted into later opportunities with law firms; and (3) the extent to which there is an opportunity to handle litigation.[17] On the first ground, civil rights programs have always attracted able young lawyers. On the second, the government's antitrust, tax, and securities lawyers have on the whole been highly competent. On the third, Justice's litigators have also been a select group.

Some agencies, of course, are able to hold out more than one of these attractions. The National Labor Relations Board comes readily to mind, and the Equal Employment Opportunity Commission has been using its new grant of litigating authority to draw lawyers who want both litigation and social change.[18] But there are some agencies whose recruiting ability will not be affected materially by a delegation of litigating authority, either because their work involves so little litigation as to be below the threshold of drawing power on this score or because their mission is so routine or unattractive to potential recruits and/or so unmarketable in the private sector as to overshadow the attractions of litigation. In the former category are such low-frequency litigants as the Central Intelligence Agency; in the latter category might be such relatively mundane, unmarketable fare as that handled by the Veterans Administration.

The point is clear: some agencies simply will not enhance their recruitment capacity significantly if they have litigation authority. Indeed, delegations to such agencies may well be counterproductive, for they may reduce the total number of able government lawyers by depleting the ranks of Justice below what they would be if the Department of Justice retained this litigation in its mix.

Some agency lawyers recognize this. One such lawyer with considerable experience dealing with Justice argues that his department has neither the time nor the talent to handle its own cases. Justice does a better job than the department might do for itself, for Justice has the better lawyers and the expertise: it "knows the circuits, the rules, the quirks, for instance what the Ninth Circuit is now doing about extensions of time."[19] Nor does he think his department could compete with the Justice Department for talent: "Every time I get a good young man I lose him to Justice. I've lost three that way. They have more responsibility, more prestige, more of everything to offer. They're an elite." Whether this particular agency lawyer is right about the relative drawing power of his department, his reservations about parceling out litigating authority underscore the problematical character of the net effect of such a delegation on the overall caliber of the federal legal establishment.

At the other extreme, a Justice Department myth also needs to be challenged. Justice can fairly be said to have a passion for uniformity of litigating position and a severe allergy to the adoption of inconsistent positions by different agencies in litigation. Administrative rationalizers, such as the Second Hoover Commission, have equally deplored diversity among departmental positions taken in court.[20] Some distinctions, however, appear in order.

First, it is one thing to have the Department of Justice itself take inconsistent positions in different cases and quite another to have two different agencies do so. Where Justice is guilty of inconsistency, its credibility with the courts suffers. But where two agencies put forward two different views of the law—each consistently maintained by that agency—this is no different from what private litigants do all the time, and yet neither the courts nor the law suffer because of the inconsistency. Indeed, an argument can be made for the benefits of diversity, both of viewpoint and context, for the judicial decision process.[21] The fear of the consequences of inconsistency ignores the fact that interagency conflicts have been resolved in court with very little impingement on other important goals for quite some time.[22]

Where uniformity is important, as I have suggested, is not so much *in* court as *after* court. The diversity that is pernicious is the diversity that stems from refusal or reluctance to follow judicial decisions or to apply their underlying spirit in a more than perfunctory way. The penchant for uniformity should find its application in counseling; it is a matter of far less urgency in litigation.

The differential impact of delegation of litigating authority on recruitment should suffice to caution against indiscriminate delegation. On the other hand, the excessiveness of concern about uniformity of litigating position should be an equally convincing argument against no delegation at all. There are one or two additional extremes that are not difficult to identify.

The first involves those agencies so beholden to client groups that, for our purposes, they could not make effective use of litigating authority if they had it. While their programs, or certain parts of them, might receive a more accurate, sympathetic airing in court, agency lawyers in essentially captive agencies would probably be helpless to set their sights much more than they presently do on judicial thinking. Decisions about what cases to defend, what cases to pursue, what cases to appeal would remain largely unaffected by the delegation of authority—except that the leavening influence of the Justice Department would be missing. Similarly, the counseling process would be unlikely to undergo any major changes in clientele-ridden agencies. The agency lawyers could not be expected to alter their perspective under such circumstances.

Agency lawyers may recognize this. On the whole, there has been little pressure from the more clientelist agencies for their own litigating authority. I pointed out in Chapter 2 that for some agencies there is considerable utility in keeping litigating authority outside the agency, so that responsibility for unfavorable or unpleasant decisions can be attributed to extramural forces. The Justice Department can be a convenient scapegoat for losses of cases in court or abandonment of cases before they get to court. In this sense, Justice is an external counterpoise to a powerful clientele that would be difficult to duplicate within the agency. If so, the present arrangements, though imperfect, may simply be the best obtainable under the circumstances. For this reason, authority to handle its own litigation should generally not be conferred on agencies that are so subject to external constituencies as virtually to be captive.

The second class of cases is more readily ascertainable. Almost without exception, it serves very little purpose to grant litigating authority to agencies with low case loads. (My only reservation on this score relates to independent regulatory commissions, not relevant here.) I said a moment ago that such delegations would probably not affect the recruitment of agency lawyers. In addition, agency legal staffs handling relatively few cases per annum would not be apt to develop the rapport with the judiciary, the ability to anticipate judge-made law, or even the familiarity with the personnel and procedure of the courts that makes delegation an appealing idea in the first place. Nor would they feel restrained about risking important doctrine for the sake of individual cases, since they have few cases to worry about. Furthermore, where litigation is a rarity, the principles involved in the lawsuits tend to be those applicable to many agencies—for example, personnel policy or freedom of information—rather than the application of program-specific rules. The latter are more likely to breed repeated litigation in the same program area. There is thus a doubly compelling case for leaving the litigation of the low-volume agencies—some of which are not necessarily small agencies—with the Department of Justice.

This immediately suggests a correlative category where a cogent case *can* be made for delegation: the agencies with high case loads whose litigation is program-specific. The frequency of their contact with the courts is apt to give rise to a high degree of learning and responsiveness to judicial norms. If their work is moderately interesting or if there is a counterpart private bar, the recruitment capacity of such agencies is likely to be improved, at least marginally, by the addition of authority over their own lawsuits. The clearest case of such a high-volume agency is the Social Security Administration, particularly in the disability benefit area. These cases usually turn on medical evidence and rarely involve principles of significance across agency lines. The expertise on this is in Social Security, not in the Justice Department, where the cases consume an amount of time disproportionate to their general importance. In the past, the courts have consistently viewed these cases rather more generously to claimants than has the Social Security Administration. There is, therefore, room for adjustment to the judicial view. With final responsibility for the litigation placed in the agency, the adjustment will probably be forthcoming, and many cases that might be litigated may well be handled administratively instead. Here, it seems to me, is a fairly clear case for delegating litigating authority.

Not all cases are so clear. As this discussion should already have suggested, what is involved is a series of tradeoffs among three clusters of variables.

The first is the likely gain or loss in agency responsiveness to the courts. For the reasons indicated earlier in this chapter, heightened agency responsiveness should be a value of prime importance in any decisions on granting or withholding litigating authority. But, as the problem of clientelism suggests, the likely gains or losses cannot be calculated across the board. The issue is not difficult to state, but it is impossible to answer a priori. The issue is whether increased responsiveness to judicial norms is achieved better by leaving litigating authority with a specialized litigation bar (Justice) that takes the courts as its reference group and is outside the agency structure. Or is responsiveness to judicial norms achieved better by making the agencies themselves responsible to the courts, so as to set up a system of countervailing pressures within the agencies?

This formulation states only implicitly what should be made explicit— that there are two variables encapsulated within the single term *responsiveness*. First, given litigating authority, will the agency lawyers develop a new sense of what the courts are aiming at, and will their understanding approach that of organizationally separate litigation lawyers? Second, if their sensitivity is increased, will it be made effective within their agencies?

The first question is essentially a matter of the capacity to adopt new orientations. If we are willing to attribute the judicial orientation of the Justice Department lawyers to their detachment—it is not *their* programs under attack, and lawyers are typically less impassioned than clients— then we may conclude that a separate litigating organization is preferable. The same conclusion follows if we attribute the sensitivity to judicial demands to the generality of the Justice Department work, to its concern with many agencies, many programs. If, however, we credit it to the litigator's experience, his having been in court repeatedly, this is a transferable trait. Give litigating responsibility to agency lawyers, at least in agencies with a certain minimum volume of litigation, and they will develop a similar relationship with the courts. Likewise, if, as Chapter 3 might suggest, some part of the divergent orientations is due to different recruitment patterns, it may be that delegation of litigating authority to some agencies will affect the composition of their legal staffs and hence their responsiveness to judicial norms.

In my view, the orientation and behavior of the Justice lawyers are attributable to all four features. As indicated, two of them (experience and recruitment) are in some cases functions of litigating authority and, therefore, transferable if that authority were to be transferred. (I shall have more to say about recruitment in a moment.) The two others (detachment and generality) derive from the fact that Justice is an organizationally separate, cross-agency litigating office. Hence these traits are not transferable to organizations lacking those characteristics. A grant of litigating authority may therefore breed greater sensitivity to the courts to the extent that it enlarges experience with the courts and alters recruitment patterns.

But the full measure of the Justice Department orientation cannot be replicated outside of a Department of Justice that has centralized litigating authority.

This still leaves the question of effectiveness in translating judicial norms into agency practice. Here, again, distinctions among agencies will manifest themselves. Much will depend on the structure of the agency and its relations with its constituencies, as I have already indicated. There may also be variations depending on the nature of its litigation, certainly on the volume and conceivably on the kind. The diversity of agency structure and business suggests a diversity of outcomes. However, it may be generally desirable, whenever litigating authority is conferred, to build in some independence for the general counsel's office—to replicate a measure of the Justice Department's organizational separateness *within* the agency—so as to enhance its capacity to respond to judicial norms and create pressures countervailing to those of interest groups and clienteles and congressional committees.

The second general variable is recruitment. Transfers of jurisdiction may well have significant effects on recruitment, though the evidence on how this works is deplorably nonexistent. Depending on the probable direction of the effect, the change can be regarded as a cost or a benefit. There is, however, a general consideration to take into account. All else being equal, there may be a professional preference for the department with the broadest jurisdiction and for the department most strongly identified with the profession—in this case, the Department of Justice on both counts. Certainly, such a preference has often been imputed to professionals by policy makers. For example, in the transfer of the Indian health program from the Department of the Interior to HEW, it was thought that physicians would be more attracted to HEW, particularly through the recruiting mechanisms of the Public Health Commissioned Corps.[23]

I note this as a general consideration lurking in the background of the litigating authority question. It argues for resolving doubts against delegation to the agenices in close cases. But, in the absence of hard evidence, it is difficult to know what weight to accord it. One reason for the ennui that sometimes results in the departure of Justice Department lawyers for the private bar or for an agency or regulatory commission is the lack of attachment to a concrete program. It may be that attracting professionals and keeping them are two different things, or that the general preference for the broadest, most professional organization is a chimera. At all events, the probable net gain or loss of legal talent to the federal bureaucracy as a whole is a consequence of change that must form part of the decision whether to transfer litigating authority or leave it where it is. As the case of the agencies with a low frequency of litigation suggests, it is possible to effect a considerable net dissipation of human resources by scattering functions to corners where able people will not follow them.

The third variable is the extent to which an agency's litigation is of a general or particular character. The more the litigation is program-specific or peculiar to the agency, the stronger is the case for delegation of litigating authority; the more general, the weaker the case.

This is true on several counts. In the first place, the more particularistic the cases, the more difficult it is for an outsider from Justice to master them and the programs from which they spring. Likewise, the narrower the litigation, the less important it is for the generalist perspective to be brought to bear on it, for the cases tend not to involve general principles. Indeed, to the extent that they do, it seems likely that, all else being equal, the agency lawyer will often appreciate their relevance to what seems to him a specialized program only after he has been to court and seen the judges at work on such cases. No amount of counseling by outsiders will suffice.

On the other side, some litigation is of so general a character as to affect the litigation of other agencies. For this, a central litigation office like Justice serves to call the attention of the courts to the implications of a seemingly narrow, one-agency, one-program decision for other agencies and other programs, thus protecting the integrity of federal administrative law, substantive as well as procedural, as it protects the interests of affected agencies not before the court. This is a traditional Department of Justice function. As I have argued earlier, the concern should be not for intragovernmental uniformity, but for the even development of the general law, the law that applies to many agencies more or less indiscriminately. Here there is a genuine case for the generalist expertise at Justice. It argues against delegation of litigating authority where the agency's litigation has a heavy component of this general quality unless the range of the agency's business is so broad as to permit within the agency the emergence of an expertise comparable to that of the Justice Department.

Unfortunately, most agencies have some of both kinds of cases—indeed, some cases have elements of both—so it is quite impossible to divide agencies neatly along this dimension. But it is even more impossible to delegate litigating authority over the one class of cases but not over the other, because the classes of cases crosscut programs and because the criteria seem incapable of precise formulation in the abstract and prospectively.

There is, however, another way of handling this: establish an office of umpire to refer cases to agencies or the Justice Department according to the criteria outlined above. The costs of such an idea, in terms of the adverse effects of an extra layer of bureaucracy and the potential for agency-Justice Department conflict over case assignments, seem greatly to outweigh any benefits that might result. On the whole, the best way to handle the issue of generality is to consider it program by program, knowing full well that there will be rough edges to any decision on whether to delegate.

This brings me to a more general point. The thrust of this discussion is rather clearly that there is no optimal solution. This is partly because the values to be maximized often conflict. Confer litigating authority on an agency with a narrow mission and recruitment may be adversely affected: a lawyer willing to handle a few such cases as part of his mix is unwilling to make them his staple diet. Certainly, both of the across-the-board alternatives—total concentration or total dispersion of litigating authority—would be likely to provide less satisfactory results, in terms of the values to be maximized, than the ad hoc method. In any event, dramatically better results may not be possible; the problem of opposite outcomes in court and agency is doubtless going to be persistent, and it is potentially, as I have maintained, quite serious.

There is, however, one drastic remedy that deserves to be discussed—namely, a fee-for-legal-services system within the federal government. There are some agencies, notably the Bureau of Standards, that provide services to other governmental units on a fee-paying basis. A legal services arrangement of this kind could presumably be devised to take advantage of market competition, by permitting agencies a choice of attorneys, private or governmental, to represent them. This, however, would almost certainly dissipate the unique knowledge of courts, judges, and the implications of judicial decisions across agencies and programs that Justice possesses. That expertise is heavily a product of the present monopoly held by the Department of Justice. The market mechanism would sacrifice it without any assurance of a corresponding gain in judicial sensitivity to agency problems or agency responsiveness to judicial concerns.

An alternative version would be to require payment of fees but without the choice of attorneys afforded by a free market. Instituting a fee system for Justice's services would no doubt require agencies to scrutinize their priorities among cases to pursue far more carefully than they now do, money costs being a factor of almost no weight in litigation decisions under the present system. But a fee system would probably do little to redress the other problems that seem to inhere in the current division of labor. Though it might make administrators reluctant to press for expensive appeals in nearly hopeless cases solely in order to place responsibility for an unpleasant decision outside the walls of the agency, a fee system would most likely also force the agencies to conduct their litigation even more closely in accordance with the wishes of powerful figures in Congress who would control their budget for legal fees. This would certainly retard responsiveness to judicial norms.

If drastic remedies do not promise equally drastic results, less drastic remedies do promise modest changes. Some improvements can be expected from ad hoc delegations, and there is every reason to experiment along these lines. The independent regulatory commissions, many of which have their own litigating authority, as well as those nonindependent agencies which also have some such authority, show that the government can survive a patchwork quilt of litigating authority, as it has survived other patchwork quilts. In the organization of the federal bureaucracy, symmetry has not been the guiding principle. If the agencies can gain a new measure of responsiveness to a judiciary playing a new role in their affairs, further sacrifices of neatness are in order.

Notes

1. J. Skelly Wright, *Beyond Discretionary Justice*, 81 YALE L. J. 575-97, 597 (Jan. 1972).

2. *Washington Post,* April 26, 1973, p. A15. The regulation related to the required distance of demonstrations from the precincts of the White House.

3. See *Administration of the Freedom of Information Act*, H. Rept. No. 92-1419, 92d Cong., 2d Sess. (1972), pp. 22-23, 26-27.

4. "Unsuitability" *dismissals* of *employees* annually run into at least the several hundreds. "Unsuitability" *rejections* of *applicants* for employment run into the thousands. Sexual misconduct was, however, only one of several potential grounds of "unsuitability," along with, for example, prior criminal record, alcoholism, and delinquency in previous employment. See *1972 Annual Report of the Civil Service Commission*, p. 73; also data from the Commission. For some illustrations of the number of cases that can be affected by a single court decision, even in an earlier day, see Homer Cummings and Carl McFarland, *Federal Justice* (New York: Macmillan, 1937), p. 503.

5. This tendency has been noted in Congress. See *U.S. Government Information Policies and Practices—Administration and Operation of the Freedom of Information Act*, Hearings Before the Subcommittee on Foreign Operations and Government Information of the Committee on Government Operations, 92d Cong., 2d Sess. (1972), pt. 4, p. 1168.

6. Paul D. Carrington, "United States Civil Appeals" (paper prepared for the Administrative Conference of the United States and the Federal Judicial Center, Feb. 28, 1973; mimeo.), p. 5.

7. Art. III, § 1.

8. Art. VI, § 2.

9. Research on the decision to litigate is now being conducted by Frank Graves of the Institute of Public Administration. *Cf.* H. Laurence

Ross, *Settled Out of Court* (Chicago: Aldine Publishing Co., 1970), pp. 163-66; Roger B. Hunting and Gloria S. Neuwirth, *Who Sues in New York City* (New York: Columbia University Press, 1962).

10. Gabriel A. Almond and Sidney Verba, *The Civic Culture* (Princeton: Princeton University Press, 1963), pp. 101-14, have called attention to the important place of faith in political institutions, outputs, and processes in a democratic order. For an example of a work suggesting by its very presence and appeal the extent of corrosion that has already occurred, see Jethro Lieberman, *How the Government Breaks the Law* (New York: Stein and Day, 1972).

11. William D. Ruckelshaus, quoted by Colman McCarthy, *Washington Post*, Jan. 29, 1974, p. A18.

12. Irving Jaffe, Acting Assistant Attorney General, Civil Division, quoted in Richard E. Cohen, "Justice Report: U.S. Attorneys Push Wide-Ranging Study to Gain Larger Role in Law Enforcement Policy," *National Journal Reports*, Vol. 5, no. 48 (Dec. 1, 1973), p. 1793.

13. For a representative view, see Robert L. Stern, *The Solicitor General's Office and Administrative Agency Litigation*, 46 A.B.A.J. 154-58, 217-18, esp. 158, 217 (Feb. 1960).

14. Cummings and McFarland, *Federal Justice*, pp. 490-91.

15. Attorney General Henry Stanbery, letter to the Senate Judiciary Committee, Dec. 20, 1867, quoted in *ibid*., p. 223.

16. Interviews, United States Postal Service, Nov. 27, 1973. *Cf*. FTC General Counsel Calvin J. Collier, quoted in Cohen, "Justice Report: U.S. Attorneys Push Study," p. 1793.

17. *Cf*. Esther Lucile Brown, *Lawyers, Law Schools and the Public Service* (New York: Russell Sage Foundation, 1948), pp. 68-70; Richard A. Solomon, *Practice of Law in the Federal Government—Career or Training Ground?*, 38 GEO. WASH. L. REV. 753-64 (May 1970).

18. Karen E. DeWitt, "Labor Report: Strengthened EEOC Accelerates Action against Business, Labor Employee Discrimination," *National Journal Reports*, Vol. 5 (June 23, 1973), pp. 913-21.

19. Interview, Nov. 13, 1973. Motions for extensions of time in which to docket cases and file briefs are among the many matters that have been handled differently, in both form and substance, from circuit to circuit.

20. Commission on the Organization of the Executive Branch of the Government, *Legal Services and Procedure: A Report to the Congress* (Government Printing Office, 1955), pp. 4, 6; *Task Force Report to Committee on Legal Services and Procedure* (Government Printing Office, 1955), pp. 59, 63-64.

21. See Note, *Government Litigation in the Supreme Court: The Roles of the Solicitor General*, 78 YALE L. J. 1442-81, at 1459-67 (July 1969).

22. See Joel E. Hoffman, *Administrative Agencies As Judicial Review Petitioners*, 25 AD. L. REV. 71-84 (Winter 1973).

23. I am indebted to David T. Stanley for the example and a helpful discussion of the general point.

Index

143

About the Author

Donald L. Horowitz, a lawyer and political scientist, has served as a government lawyer and as law clerk to a federal judge. He has also held research appointments at the Harvard University Center for International Affairs, the Woodrow Wilson International Center for Scholars, and the Brookings Institution. Currently senior fellow at the Smithsonian Institution's Research Institution on Immigration and Ethnic Studies, Dr. Horowitz is the author of *The Courts and Social Policy* (Brookings, 1976).